THE
Holy
Spirit

THE

Holy

Spirit

A Layman's Perspective

Don and Jackie Ragland

Providence House Publishers
PROVIDENCE PUBLISHING CORPORATION
FRANKLIN, TENNESSEE

Printed in the United States of America

09   08   07   06   05   1   2   3   4   5

Library of Congress Control Number: 2005909030

ISBN: 1-57736-357-4

Cover design by Joey McNair

PROVIDENCE HOUSE PUBLISHERS
an imprint of
Providence Publishing Corporation
238 Seaboard Lane • Franklin, Tennessee 37067
www.providence-publishing.com
800-321-5692

To the Spirit
of
the risen Christ
who lives in our hearts,
and
to all who seek Him.

❄ *Contents* ❄

⊰ *Foreword* ⊱

I met Dr. Don Ragland fourteen years ago and immediately liked him. From the start we developed a relationship that would bring us together in a powerful and wonderful way. That relationship was fueled by the fire and power of the Holy Spirit. The Holy Spirit was the catalyst for a tremendous outpouring of love and power that occurred throughout the Middle Tennessee area. Much of that revival can be traced back to workshops that Don shared in local churches which introduced hundreds to the third person of the Trinity.

What you have in your hands is a result of these life-changing workshops. I was present at many of them and watched firsthand as this wonderful, spirit-filled layman introduced churches to the power of the Holy Spirit. It was introduced simply yet profoundly. As a result, whole congregations were able to be challenged and directed to be disciples of Jesus Christ. Don Ragland and his wife, Jackie, have dedicated their lives to seeing the Holy Spirit introduced in the local church. This book is a wonderful tool in living out what the Holy Spirit will and can do in the life of the church.

Read this book, and then read it again, and you will be as blessed as I have been to be in intimate fellowship with the Holy Spirit.

Rev. Thomas E. Halliburton
United Methodist Church

✢ *Preface* ✢

Over the past fourteen years, God has seen fit to allow me the opportunity to travel to different churches throughout Middle Tennessee and share His teachings about the Holy Spirit. In this book, I give details of how God brought me to the point of having this opportunity. I have taught this seminar in Methodist, Baptist, Assemblies of God, and nondenominational churches. I have shared with groups as large as two hundred and as small as six and across different cultures. The one constant over all these years has been the hunger I have seen in people for more of God: a desire to know the power of God in their everyday lives.

So many good Christian people live lives that are spiritually powerless. They seem to be unable to overcome their own sinful tendencies and addictions, even though they may strongly desire to do so. They end up living "double lives": they know the kind of lives they should strive for but are unable to attain them. After years of living like this, many become frustrated, joyless, and bitter. Some reject their faith altogether as not being relevant to the problems of this life and see belief in Jesus as little more than an insurance policy to provide for the afterlife. They have responded to the truth of the gospel and accepted Jesus as Savior, but, just as those disciples whom Paul found in Ephesus, they have never even heard of the Holy Spirit (Acts 19:1–7). What little others know of the Spirit is limited to their exposure to televangelists.

God gave me a heart to share the message of the Comforter in such a way that people would want to know Him and experience Him daily. I am a layman in the church, a veterinarian by profession. Being a layman, it seems that people can some-times relate to me in certain ways more easily than they can with a member of the clergy. They look at me and think, "If he finds this stuff important as a veterinarian, maybe there's some-thing in it for me." I'm not a theologian and don't pretend to be. I'm simply a man who responded to the wooing of the Holy Spirit as a young boy, accepted Jesus as my Savior, and have been abundantly blessed by Him throughout my life. Oh, there have been times when I have strayed away from Him, and life has had its normal ups and downs, blessings and difficulties, but He has always been there.

I never intended to put these teachings into book form. They first started out as a series of Sunday school lessons for an adult class I was teaching. (I'm still teaching that same class and many of the same people after almost twenty years! They deserve a medal for putting up with my ramblings and musings over all those years.)

One of the members of my class, who had taught the class before me, had been not only my Sunday school teacher but my eleventh grade English teacher as well. She had been baptized in the Holy Spirit a few years prior to my beginning to teach this class. After hearing these lessons on the Spirit, she said something to me that proved to be a prophetic utterance: "These lessons are for a broader audience." Not long after-ward, the doors began to open for me so that I might share with various churches. The lessons changed and evolved some over time as my own understanding and experience grew, but the theme has always been the same: God has provided a way for us to live powerful, fulfilled, and victorious Christian lives. Just like those we read about in the New Testament, we can know the indwelling presence of Christ and have the inner assurance of our salvation. God wants us to experience His salvation daily, not just know about Him intellectually.

Some people in my workshops began to ask for notes or handouts of the teaching. I eventually developed a PowerPoint presentation for use during the seminar. But I still had no urge to write a book. Over the past two years, however, everywhere I taught people kept asking if I had these lessons available in book form. When I explained that I did not, they were always encouraging me to write the book. My wife was also encouraging me to do so. I finally began to feel that maybe the Lord was trying to tell me that it was time to make the commitment to record these teachings in a more permanent form. That's how this book came to be.

I asked Jackie, my lovely wife of twenty-eight years, to write the last chapter. I wanted the reader to get her perspective of what this relationship to Jesus by the Spirit has meant to our family. It has been almost twenty-two years as of this writing since she and I both first received the filling of the Spirit. I cannot imagine (and have no desire to know!) what those years would have been like without walking daily with the Holy Spirit. He has been our constant guide, comfort, and source of wisdom in running our home and business, as well as in rearing our children.

My goal in writing this book is simple. I want the Lord to do with it as He wishes. I pray that I have been obedient in writing it. I pray that He has enabled me to write a book that is simple and easily understood. As you find yourself reading this, I pray your efforts are worthwhile. Perhaps in reading these words, the Holy Spirit can spark a new love for Jesus in your heart, and you will be encouraged to give yourself more completely to Him. Perhaps these passages will enable you to share your faith more easily with others. If you have not known the Spirit before, maybe He can use something in these pages to prompt you to ". . . taste and see that the Lord is good" (Ps. 34:8). God bless!

⚔ *Acknowledgments* ⚔

I really don't know how to begin to thank everyone whom I should. God has blessed my life with so many people through whom my faith has been birthed and nurtured. It would be impossible for me to remember everybody for whom I should be thankful, so first let me apologize to those I fail to mention specifically.

First and foremost is Jesus; without Him there would be no meaning to life. My parents, Willie and Frances Ragland, are faithful Christians who ensured we went to church regularly as a family, and they have always been good examples by their unselfish lives. They lived out the instruction of the Bible to raise their children in the nurture and admonition of the Lord.

Over the years, my life has been enriched by a host of other people who gave of themselves as youth group leaders, pastors, Sunday school teachers, and friends. Lucille Hyder has been a teacher, counselor, and friend for thirty years. God has used her as a powerful spiritual influence in my life, and her influence continues even today as we attend the same church and Sunday school class.

Tom Halliburton, my former pastor, current district superintendent, and friend, has been a tremendous encouragement to me. His dedication and passion for serving the Lord are contagious. He has traveled with me for hundreds of miles in support of my teaching and has spent hours with me in prayer ministry.

My current pastor, Craig Green, has also shown me a passion and love for Jesus that have encouraged me to "press on," and he has challenged me in being open to fresh, new ways to spread the gospel.

Pat Grimes is my longtime friend and confidant. Pat and I have shared the beauty of the outdoors together on many miles of hiking and canoeing and spent many nights camping with our kids. He has been a thoughtful sounding board for my spiritual queries and discoveries, and I have never known a more generous soul.

Tom Riley and Rick Wearing are my business partners and Christian friends. Their hard work, along with the other doctors and staff in our practice, has allowed me to have time to devote to this project.

Without the generosity of Stan and Patrice Randolph, who allowed me to use their lake cabin retreat, I would never have found the quiet hours necessary to write. My sister, Brenda Lewis, was gracious to lend her time and talents in editing this manuscript. She is a very dedicated and talented English professor as well as a kind and loving person.

My family has endured many inconveniences over the years due to my professional life. The schedule of a rural veterinarian is unpredictable at best. Add to that all of the hours spent in preparation, traveling, and teaching for the Lord and you already know that I have one of the most understanding wives imaginable. For over twenty-eight years, Jackie has been my best friend, faithful companion, love of my life, mother of my kids, prayer partner, and dedi-cated sister in Christ. I cannot imagine having traveled this life without her.

To my three sons, Jared, Eric, and Paul, I just thank you for understanding why Daddy wasn't always home. What a joy it has been to watch each of you come to your own faith in Jesus and grow up as strong Christian young adults. You make me proud.

To Niquie, Jared's wife and my daughter-in-law, I want to express my thanks and joy that God has honored us by bringing such a fine Christian young lady into our family to help carry on the faith to the following generations.

To my many friends and members together in the body of Christ, I thank you for allowing me to see Jesus in you. May we continue this journey of faith together until the Lord returns or we all go home in victory. God richly bless you each and every one!

⚹ *Chapter 1* ⚹
Who Is the Holy Spirit?

W ho is the Holy Spirit? Many people's response to this question, including that of many Christians, is to think of something mystical and impossible to understand. Their thoughts immediately go to various things they have seen or heard about manifestations of this Spirit, including healing services and speaking in tongues. However, the Holy Spirit is not some "thing" invented at the first Pentecost after the resurrection of Jesus. He is not goose bumps. He is not speaking in tongues. He is not falling on the floor. He is not shouting. He is not healing or miracles. We sometimes react to His presence in these ways or see Him manifested in these events, but these evidences of His presence do not explain who He is. He is not some unknowable, ethereal force for good in the universe that floats around "doing good." The Holy Spirit has been present since the beginning and will be forever.

The Spirit has been active in the affairs of creation since before the foundations of the earth. In the first chapter of the first book of the Bible, we see Him at work: "In the beginning God created the heavens and the earth. And the earth was without form and void and darkness covered the face of the deep. And the Spirit of God moved upon the face of the waters" (Gen. 1:1–2). When God confirmed His covenant with Abraham, the Holy Spirit was present, moving through the midst of the covenant sacrifices as a burning torch (Gen. 15:17). As God gave the commandments to Moses on Mount Sinai, the words on the tablets of stone were written by the "finger of God" (Gen. 31:18).

Approximately fourteen hundred years later, Jesus explained that He cast out demons by the "finger of God" (Luke 11:20) or, as named in the parallel account in Matthew, the "Spirit of God" (Matt. 12:28). As Samuel anointed Saul to become the first king of Israel, the Holy Spirit came upon him (1 Sam. 10:6). Later, when Saul sinned in rebellion against God, the Scriptures tell us that the Spirit departed from him (1 Sam. 16:14). This sudden void left Saul in such a state of desperation that he sought spiritual advice from the witch at En Dor (1 Sam. 28:7–8).

When Samuel anointed David to become the next king, the Scripture plainly says that the Holy Spirit came upon David, empowering him for this position (1 Sam. 16:13). David later sinned in having Uriah killed and taking Bathsheba as his wife. When confronted with this sin by the prophet Nathan, David repented with these words: "Create in me a clean heart, O God, and renew a right spirit within me. Cast me not away from thy presence: take not thy Holy Spirit from me. Restore unto me the joy of thy salvation; and uphold me with thy free Spirit" (Ps. 51:10–12 KJV). David had watched Saul's demise, and he understood that without the Holy Spirit he would have neither the wisdom nor the strength to be king. Likewise, without the Spirit, he would have no joy in life.

Throughout the Old Testament, we continue to see the Spirit working actively in the lives of the prophets, priests, and kings. Likewise, in the New Testament, this activity continues as we see Mary conceived with child by the power of the Holy Spirit (Luke 1:35). Later Jesus Himself is filled with the Spirit at His baptism and is thereafter continually led by that same Spirit (Luke 3:22, 4:1). He was later resurrected from the grave by the power of the Spirit (Rom. 8:11) and presented himself before His Father in Heaven by the power of the "eternal Spirit" (Heb. 9:14).

The book of Acts chronicles the lives of the early followers of Jesus as they are filled with and led by the Holy Spirit, spreading the gospel through word and action. The letters of the New Testament are filled with information regarding the relationship of believers to the Holy Spirit. The last chapter of the last book of the Bible shows the Holy Spirit working with the "bride" as they pray together for the return of the Lord Jesus (Rev. 22:17).

Very literally, from the first book to the last book of the Holy Scriptures, from the opening verses to the closing verses, we see the Spirit at work. From before the beginning of recorded human history until the predicted end of history as we know it, the Spirit of God is and will continue to be active in the affairs of creation.

A reasonable description of the Spirit might be the manifestation of God that works intimately with His creation. God the Father is enthroned in heaven, and we cannot at this time be with Him face to face. Jesus, God the Son, is currently seated at the right hand of the Father, interceding on our behalf as High Priest and awaiting the time of His physical

> *God the Spirit . . . never leaves us for an instant but is our ever-present guide, teacher, comforter, counselor, and friend.*

return to Earth at the end of this age. While He does exist in a resurrected and glorified body, Jesus is not physically present with us at this time. God the Spirit, however, is with us continuously and closely. He never leaves us for an instant but is our ever-present guide, teacher, comforter, counselor, and friend. He is the Spirit of Jesus and our constant companion.

Who is the Holy Spirit?
The Spirit of the risen
Christian who lives
in my heart.

The best definition of the Holy Spirit which I have heard came from a young girl in Sunday school class. When asked, "Who is the Holy Spirit?" her reply was, "the Spirit of the risen Christ who lives in my heart." This simple statement contains the answer to a question which has been pondered for ages, a mystery hidden for generations.

This mystery is spoken of in the Scriptures. First Corinthians 2:1–7 tells us that Satan and the forces of darkness would never have crucified the "Lord of Glory" had they foreseen the victory which God accomplished through the crucifixion and resurrection. This mystery was hidden from their wisdom. They were unable to discern that through apparent defeat in death, Christ provided the way for a New Covenant in which the law of God was no longer written on tablets of stone but within the very hearts of His people (Jer. 31:33). Ephesians 3:9–11 states that this mystery is revealed through the church, and Colossians 1:27 reveals the answer to this ages-old mystery: "Christ in you, the hope of glory." The Spirit of the risen Christ who lives in my heart!

Near the end of His earthly ministry, Jesus spoke to the disciples about the coming of the Spirit. We can learn much about Him by looking at some of these passages of Scripture (John 14:16–18, 25–26, 15:26, 16:7–15). Jesus assured His disciples that after He was gone, He would send another Comforter to be with them. He would not leave them alone. Indeed, it was for their benefit that He was going away, for the Comforter could not come unless Jesus first went the way of the cross. He further assured them that they would know this Spirit when He arrived because He had already dwelt with them and they would be able to recognize Him when He returned.

How had the Spirit been dwelling with the disciples? In Jesus, of course, for He was given the Spirit in all fullness (John 3:34). How would the disciples recognize the Spirit when He came back to them? They would see in Him the same personality they had come to know in Jesus. He would like what Jesus had liked, minister as Jesus had ministered, heal as Jesus had healed, and love as Jesus had loved. There would be no difference between the personality and ministry of the Holy Spirit and the personality and ministry of Jesus Christ.

The disciples, having come to know Jesus and having spent time with Him, would be able to recognize the Holy Spirit because there would be absolutely no difference in their presence. There would be one important difference, however, in the relationship between the disciples and the Holy Spirit. Jesus had dwelt *among* them, but when He came back, the Spirit would dwell *in* them. "Christ in you, the hope of glory"; the Spirit of the risen Christ who lives in my heart!

Remember, if Satan could have foreseen this wonder, he would rather have let Jesus live than risk the power of God that was released into the world through His death. God's light, unleashed through millions of believers throughout ages to come, was and is released into Satan's realm of darkness. Consider that if Satan takes this work of God so seriously, perhaps we Christians take it too lightly for the most part. God has provided the means to take the gospel to all the nations and preach, teach, heal, and bring deliverance to those held captive in the world of darkness. He greatly desires that we use this gift of His Spirit. He died to make it possible.

John 16:13–15 tells about the work of the Spirit and how the Spirit takes of those things which are Christ's and shares them with us. Just as Jesus revealed the nature of the Father, the Holy Spirit reveals Christ to those who seek Him. During the time that Jesus was on Earth, the chosen people of God had become so far removed from the true nature of God that most could not recognize Him when He actually came to them. Jesus' exasperation with this can be seen in His response when, near the end of His earthly ministry, Philip asked Him to show them the Father. "Have I been so long time with you, and yet hast thou not known me, Philip? He that hath seen me hath seen the Father . . ." (John 14:8–9 KJV).

> *It is impossible to separate the work of the Spirit from the work of Jesus.*
>
> ❖

Today, many children of God have again failed to come to know the true nature of God. We know much *about* God, but often we do not *know Him*. We too often focus our faith on the observances of tradition and ritual to the virtual exclusion of the presence of God. We know our religion much better than we know Jesus. However, the presence of the Holy Spirit makes this error unnecessary.

Alternately, some believers wish to substitute praise and worship for a true relationship with the Holy Spirit, mistaking the exultation they get from worship as the fullness of the Spirit. It is very appropriate and necessary that we praise and worship the living God, but we must never mistake our feelings as the deeper presence and truth of God. We must allow the Holy Spirit to use these experiences of His presence to further sanctify and perfect us through repentance, healing, deliverance, and grace.

It is impossible to separate the work of the Spirit from the work of Jesus. The two are One. It is only a delusion if we think we can follow Jesus without following the direction and revelation of the Spirit. It is equally erroneous to think that the goal of our faith is to be found in the gifts and manifestations of the Spirit. The goal of our faith is to be found in the person of Jesus and the impartation of the divine nature to us through the promise of His indwelling Spirit (2 Pet. 1:3–4).

It is folly to divide the church into camps based upon whether we are following the Spirit or following Christ. It is impossible to truly follow one without the other. A faith that focuses primarily on manifestations of the Spirit is misguided, for the Spirit "speak[s] not of himself" but glorifies Jesus (John 16:13–14). Remember, miraculous signs follow believers; believers are not supposed to chase after signs and wonders (Mark 16:17). It is only through the Spirit of Truth that we can come to fully know Jesus.

Who is the Holy Spirit? He is God with us. He is Christ in you. He is the Spirit of Life, the Spirit of Light, the Spirit of Righteousness, the Spirit of Truth, the Comforter, the Counselor, and the Teacher. He is the Spirit of the risen Christ who lives in our hearts.

Questions for Reflection

1. How long has the Holy Spirit been present?

2. Where do we first see the Holy Spirit at work in Scripture?

3. Who is "the finger of God?" Why is He so named?

4. Is there evidence of the Holy Spirit's work in the life of King David? Explain.

5. Where do we first see the work of the Holy Spirit in the New Testament?

6. Where can we see the Holy Spirit at work in the life of Jesus?

7. Are there further accounts of the work of the Holy Spirit after Jesus' death and resurrection?

8. Who is the Holy Spirit?

9. How were the disciples to recognize the Spirit when He came to them?

10. What is the work of the Holy Spirit?

11. How can we come to know God rather than know about God?

12. What is the goal of our faith as followers (believers) of Jesus Christ?

13. Would the Holy Spirit be more accurately referred to as a "person" or a "thing?"

14. What are the major differences in the "anointing" of the Spirit under the Old Covenant and the "indwelling" of the Spirit in the New Covenant?

❧ Chapter 2 ❧
Something More

T he years 1982 and 1983 were hard years in the life of my then-young family. There was certainly nothing going on that was particularly unique or more difficult than what happens to most folks at some point in their lives. However, if allowed, God uses these times in our lives to get our attention and turn our thoughts toward Him. That is exactly what happened to Jackie and me.

In searching for some purpose for our lives and the cause of these problems we were facing, we both sought God with renewed vigor. Having been reared in the church and having accepted Christ as a young boy, I was well versed in Bible stories and the morality of the Christian life. I understood that a personal relationship with Jesus was possible through the salvation He purchased on the cross. But in the ensuing years, I had come to know many good people who were not Christians. These associations had caused some inward questioning of my faith.

My years in professional school and my new career in veterinary medicine were very demanding. Jackie was suffering from major depression. The future of our marriage was in jeopardy. I seemed to have lost the capacity to extend or experience emotional affection. I was no longer sure that the God I had known either could or would meet the present needs of our lives.

One night in great distress I remember telling God that I was no longer sure that this Christian life was worth all the time and effort. If there was something more than I had known of my relationship to Him, He had better show me; otherwise, I was going to forget all of it and concentrate my time and energies on other endeavors.

I began to search the Scriptures in earnest to find out for myself if there was indeed something more. Of course, God is faithful even when we are not. When given a chance, He will always make Himself known. He did indeed show me the answers for which I was seeking by introducing me to the one manifestation of Himself of whom I was unaware: the Holy Spirit.

The Trinity is a truth that is taught throughout the Scriptures, although the exact nature of the triune God is not taught. Theologians have long pondered this question, and it is certainly beyond my understanding and ability to explain the exact relationship between God the Father, God the Son, and God the Spirit. This is a concept my mind cannot fully comprehend, yet it would be foolish to reject a truth so clearly taught in the Scriptures merely because there is something about that truth I cannot understand. If I could understand everything about God with my mind, then God would never be any larger than my limited understanding. Thus, it should come as no surprise that a finite intellect cannot fully comprehend an infinite God. The more I think about it, the more I realize that I want a God who is much bigger than what my limited brain can comprehend. However, we can gain some insight into the nature of God as we study the Scriptures regarding the working of the Spirit in the life of Jesus.

> *God is faithful even when we are not.*

❖

The gospel of Luke records that Mary, while still a virgin, conceived by the power of the Holy Spirit and gave birth to Jesus. The Spirit came upon the baby in the womb of Mary's cousin Elizabeth and empowered him to become the earthly forerunner of Christ known as John the Baptist (Luke 1:30–44). Next, the Spirit anointed Simeon and allowed him to understand that Mary's baby presented for dedication was the promised deliverer of Israel.

We are told very little about Jesus in His early years. It is recorded that He "grew, waxed strong in spirit, filled with wisdom: and the grace of God was upon him" (Luke 2:25–40). When Jesus was thirty years old, He was baptized in the Jordan River by His cousin John. This marked the beginning of His public ministry.

Scriptures record that when John baptized Jesus with water, "the heaven was opened, and the Holy Ghost descended in bodily shape like a dove upon him . . ." (Luke 3:21–22), thus fulfilling the prophecy given to John concerning the coming Lamb of God. The Father spoke from heaven at this time, "You are my beloved Son; in You I am well pleased" (Luke 3:22).

Immediately after this, Jesus is said to be "full of the Holy Spirit" (Luke 4:1). Jesus was conceived by the Holy Spirit, and we know that the Spirit of God had always been with Him. What was different in their relationship that He was now said to be "full" of the Spirit? The answer lies in what happens next.

Jesus was immediately led by the Spirit into the wilderness for a time of temptation prior to beginning His ministry. This is the first time Scripture gives any indication that Jesus was specifically led by the Spirit to some particular place or action. After the wilderness temptation, He returned in the "power of the Spirit" (Luke 4:14) and He officially announced His anointing by the Spirit to preach, heal, and deliver. He further stated that this Scripture was fulfilled "this day" (Luke 4:21).

Being filled with the Spirit seems to be synonymous with having the power of the Spirit operating in His life.

From this time on, Jesus' life was spent doing exactly what the Spirit led Him to do. Jesus stated repeatedly that the works He did were not His own, but the Father's. And the words He spoke were not His own, but the Father's. I believe that God's desire for all His children is found in this relationship between His Son and His Spirit. Jesus was *born* of the Spirit at conception, *filled* with the Spirit at His baptism, and *walked* in the power of the Spirit the rest of His life.

Peter's understanding of Jesus seems to place great importance on this relationship. On the day of Pentecost, when explaining to the crowd about the outpouring of the Holy Spirit, Peter presents Jesus to the crowd as "a man approved by God among you by miracles and wonders and signs . . ." (Acts 2:22). Later, when sharing the gospel with Cornelius, Peter explains that "God anointed Jesus of Nazareth with the Holy Spirit and with power,

> *Jesus was* **born** *of the Spirit at conception,* **filled** *with the Spirit at His baptism, and* **walked** *in the power of the Spirit the rest of His life.*

who went about doing good and healing all who were oppressed by the devil, for God was with Him" (Acts 10:38).

In each case Peter could have correctly identified Jesus simply as the Christ, the Son of God, or the Messiah. But he chooses to emphasize the humanity of Jesus dependent upon the Holy Spirit: a man empowered by the Spirit of God to do the work of God. Jesus as the Son of Man shows us what the Father has provided for His children: man in intimate relationship with his Heavenly Father through the Holy Spirit. Jesus was indeed born of the Spirit, filled with the Spirit, and walked in the power of the Spirit.

Discussing this relationship with the Holy Spirit creates many questions as we strive to understand the role of the Spirit in our own lives. We may wonder, *Does this relationship apply to ordinary men and women like me?* Scripture reveals the same pattern in the lives of the disciples.

On the evening of the Resurrection, Jesus appears to His followers who are gathered behind locked doors for fear of the Jewish religious leaders. The resurrected Lord appears, breathes on them, and says, "Receive ye the Holy Spirit" (John 20:22). [The "breath of God" is simply another name for the Holy Spirit (Gen. 2:7; Job 33:4). The Greek *pneumos* is translated both "breath" and "spirit."] What happened to the disciples at this time? Would it not seem logical that they received eternal life from Jesus?

Prior to this time, no one could be born of the Spirit and enter the Kingdom of God because of sin. Not until Jesus died on the cross as a sacrifice for the sins of all men was this possible. On the first day after rising victoriously out of the grave, He returned to those faithful few and bestowed upon them the greatest gift of all: new birth and new life in the Spirit. When Jesus breathed upon them, they were "born of the Spirit" just as Jesus had earlier explained to Nicodemus (John 3:1–5).

For the next forty days, Jesus appeared at various times to them and spoke to them concerning the Kingdom of God. One can only imagine the wonder they felt as they sat at His feet, seeing His glorified body, listening to His explanations of things past, present, and future. How excited they must have been and how anxious to share this miraculous news with all the people they knew. Conversely, they must have been somewhat confused when Jesus instructed them not to go anywhere, but rather to wait in Jerusalem until they had received the promise of the Father—the baptism of the Holy Spirit (Acts 1:1–5).

Had they not been previously anointed with this same Spirit to perform miracles and cast out demons? Had Jesus Himself not conveyed spiritual birth to them forty days ago? What were they waiting for? Ten days later, when gathered in the Upper Room, their questions were answered as the Spirit moved upon them as a mighty wind and flames of fire. They were now filled with the Spirit just as Jesus had been in the Jordan River.

The rest of the book of Acts records the disciples being led by the Holy Spirit as they proclaimed the gospel of Jesus to people. They preached, taught, healed, delivered, and spread the news of salvation in the power of the Holy Spirit—just as Jesus had. They were *born of the Spirit, baptized with the Spirit, and walked in the power of the Spirit.*

These were, however, people who had been very close to Jesus in the flesh. They were eyewitnesses of the Resurrection. Would this same pattern apply to all who would receive Jesus? Peter's sermon on that Pentecost day seems to imply that it would, for he states clearly that ". . . the promise is to you and to your children, and to all who are afar off, as many as the Lord our God will call" (Acts 2:39).

Following the stoning of Stephen, the early Christians began to disperse from Jerusalem. As they went to various communities and nations, they continued to share the Good News of Jesus. Philip went to Samaria (Acts 8:5–17). He talked to them of Jesus' death and resurrection and performed many miracles in their sight. The people received the news of Jesus, believed in Him, and were baptized. Today we would say they were saved or born again.

What was the response of the church leaders when this wonderful news arrived in Jerusalem? They immediately dispatched Peter and John for the express purpose of making sure these new believers received the baptism of the Holy Spirit. How important they must have considered this to be! This passage makes absolutely clear the distinction between being *born* of the Spirit and being *baptized* with the Spirit. Salvation was only the beginning. The new birth was just that, a birth—a beginning.

> *The disciples were* **born** *of the Spirit,* **baptized** *with the Spirit, and* **walked** *in the power of the Spirit.*
>
> ❡

The next needful step was to receive the power to grow—the baptism of the Spirit. Just as Jesus told the disciples not to leave Jerusalem until they had been clothed with this heavenly power, they understood that all new believers in Jesus would need this same empowerment and were faithful to fulfill their duty to the new converts.

The account of Peter's sharing the gospel with Cornelius and his household in Acts 10 and Paul's discovery of the band of twelve disciples in Ephesus in Acts 19 give similar testimony to the importance which the early church placed upon both the new birth (i.e., receiving Jesus) and the baptism of the Holy Spirit. The Scriptures clearly show the pattern extended to all believers, exactly as Peter had said.

Born of the Spirit; baptized with the Spirit; walking in the Spirit: this progression is what God has provided for all those who love Him. To accept anything less would be to fall short of God's desire for our lives. To accept anything less would be to fall prey to Satan's lies. To accept anything less would be to live a frustrated life knowing the truth of salvation but having no power to live victoriously as the Scriptures describe. To accept anything less would be to miss the "something more" for which my heart was longing. I began to understand! "Please God," I prayed, "Grant me the grace to receive your Spirit!"

Questions for Reflection

1. What is meant by the Trinity?

2. Can we fully comprehend an infinite God? Why or why not?

3. When was Jesus "born" of the Spirit?

4. When was Jesus "filled" with the Holy Spirit? What was His reaction?

5. How was Jesus different after this point?

6. Why did Peter emphasize Jesus' humanity while preaching on the day of Pentecost?

7. When were Jesus' disciples born of the Spirit? When were they filled with the Spirit?

8. Was the work of the Holy Spirit in Jesus' life completed after Jesus was "filled" or baptized? In the disciples' lives?

9. This pattern suggests a progression in the lives of Jesus and His disciples. What is this progression? Does it apply to us today?

10. What types of difficulties might Christians expect in their lives if they fail to mature in their relationship with the Holy Spirit?

⊀ *Chapter 3* ⊁
Born of the Spirit

T o understand what it means to be born of the Spirit, we must have some idea what it means to be dead to the Spirit. The Scriptures give us great insight into who we are as created human beings and how we arrived at the condition in which we now find ourselves. In closing his letter to the church at Thessalonica, Paul writes that he desires for God to "sanctify" them completely; that they be wholly set apart by God for His purposes; that their entire being—body, soul, and spirit—be thus affected by their heavenly Father (1 Thess. 5:23). This simple verse opens the door to a wonderful truth about humankind. We are beings who are composed of three main parts: body, soul, and spirit.

Unless otherwise instructed, most people will tell you that people consist of a body and soul. Some others would say body and spirit, assuming the soul and spirit to be synonymous. However, these responses are not accurate according to the Scriptures. Each of our three parts, although intimately inter-twined, has a distinct function. Obviously, humans are terribly complex, and anything that greatly affects one part of our being will consequently influence the other parts as well. However, it has proven very enlightening to come to an under-standing of the major characteristics of each part. By better understanding ourselves, it becomes easier to understand how the Holy Spirit relates to us. Let us briefly explore each of these parts.

The body is perhaps the easiest of the parts to understand. It is what we see when we look at each other. It is through the physical senses that we relate to the world around us. Our bodies are first conceived in the womb, begin to be fashioned according to pattern by the miracle of DNA, and are born into this world small, wrinkled, and all but helpless. We grow and change over time. We get bigger, stronger, less wrinkled, and more independent. Our bodies put great demand upon our lives, and a large portion of our lives is devoted to taking care of our bodies' needs. Eventually, barring some early demise, our bodies become smaller, weaker, more wrinkled, and more dependent once again. The body finally dies and decays, becoming part of the environment as it is slowly reduced to basic elements (i.e., "ashes to ashes, dust to dust").

Our bodies are important for sure, but they are not the real us. Bodies do change over time. Through illness, injury, or surgery they may change drastically in a short period of time. While bodily changes sometimes call for emotional changes and readjustments, our bodies do not truly define who we are. Consider identical twins who share strikingly similar bodies, yet each remains a unique individual. Our uniqueness is defined not by our bodies but by our souls.

In both the Hebrew and Greek understanding (the two primary original languages of the Bible), it is the soul that is the sum of each individual personality. Of all the billions of human souls that have existed, there has never been another soul like yours, nor will there ever be. Your soul makes you uniquely who you are. This one-of-a-kind combination of intellect, emotion, and will gives you a personality that is completely and individually yours. You are a unique creation of God.

The soul, by its own nature, is self-centered, self-aware, and self-concerned. This is necessary for your protection and the propagation of the species. This "living soul" enables us to have ideals and aspirations. It enables us to dream and learn and grow. This self-centered tendency of the soul is useful and proper as long as it is kept in submission to the spirit. If not held in balance, however, this natural tendency becomes very destructive.

In Christian thinking, the soul is preserved forever. Once conceived, your soul will continue to exist forever. It may exist in God's presence or in His absence, but it never ceases to be. We are given many instances in the Scriptures of the preservation of the uniqueness of the soul long after the body has died. We see Moses and Elijah on the Mount of Transfiguration hundreds of years after their deaths (or in Elijah's case, transformation). We are told that, at his death, the beggar Lazarus was carried into Abraham's bosom. We are likewise told that we will sit down at the heavenly wedding feast with Abraham, Isaac, and Jacob. This could not be possible if the individuality of the soul were lost at death.

If the body is merely the means by which we relate to the physical world and the soul is defined by our unique personality, what is the spirit? The Scriptures indicate that the spirit is what makes human beings unique from the other creatures that God has created. When God breathed into Adam's body (formed from the earth) the breath of life, Adam became a "living soul" (Gen. 2:7 KJV): a soul with life. Whose life? God's life.

God desired to create man in His own image, after His own likeness. This creation required that the very life of God be imparted to man to make man a creature of eternity; to elevate the soul of man to a higher plane than the souls of the other animals; to enable him to communicate with and fellowship with the eternal God. It is the spark of God's uncreated life breathed into man that makes us eternal beings.

The spirit breathed into man is the part of us that has direct communion with God and was intended to be the predominant guiding force of our lives. The spirit, by its nature, is God-centered and God-seeking. Before the fall, Adam and Eve had fellowship with God daily and did His directed work upon the Earth. The desires of their minds and hearts and the actions of their bodies were in direct submission to and in perfect harmony with God's Spirit.

God had provided for all their needs but had also allowed for the exercise of their free will by allowing access to the Tree of Knowledge in the Garden of Eden. He instructed them that "in the day" that they ate of this tree, they would die (Gen. 2:17). Satan, disguised as the serpent, contradicted this statement when he told Eve "You will not surely die" (Gen. 3:4). Who told the truth? They both did.

God and Satan were speaking from vastly different points of view and for greatly different reasons. God was seeking to protect Adam and Eve. Satan was seeking to destroy them. Did Adam and Eve die physically the day they disobeyed God? The fact is they lived for hundreds of years after being expelled from the Garden. Did their souls cease to exist on the day they sinned? No! As a matter of fact, in a sense, their souls were enlarged and magnified. The statement of Satan became true. Their "eyes were opened" and they became "like gods" to know "good and evil" (Gen. 3:7, 22).

Satan told the truth—to a certain extent. They did not die physically, and they did not lose their individuality that day. What did they lose? They lost spiritual communion with their Creator. Upon having their eyes opened, they were ashamed and were no longer comfortable in God's presence. They tried to cover their nakedness and hid from the presence of God (Gen. 3:7–8). They had suffered a spiritual death and were no longer one with their Lord (1 Cor. 6:17).

Since their spirits were no longer in harmony with God's Spirit, their spirits were no longer the strongest parts of their beings. Instead, their souls became the dominant force in their lives. Their eyes were opened to know good and evil, and they were now held in the grip of "the lust of the flesh, the lust of the eyes, and the pride of life" (1 John 2:16). The death of their spirits pervaded all of their being, and their bodies became mortal and subject to pain and death. Their minds lost the ability to know the mind of God. Their hearts

> *All of the man-made religions, philosophies, and belief systems have been our attempt to get back to God.*

lost the desire for the goodness of God. Their wills lost the humility to be submissive to God. Acting out of His mercy, God did not destroy them but removed them from the Garden so they would no longer have access to the Tree of Life and be able to live forever in a fallen state (Gen. 3:22–24).

Adam and Eve later had children who were born like them (Gen. 5:3). That is, they were born with very alive bodies and souls, but dead spirits, spirits not in communion with their Creator and with no power to direct their lives. All men born since, except Jesus, have been born in this likeness (Rom. 5:12–21). This fact is readily observable. The body is definitely mortal and subject to death.

The natural tendency of man is to be self-centered, thus indicating that man's own soul is naturally in charge of his life. Do you have to teach a two-year-old child to share his toys or to be selfish? Of course, you have to teach him how to share. We would think it strange otherwise, since we consider it natural for a young child to be selfish; that is, we expect that, by nature, a young child will seek the fulfillment of his own needs. Do you have to teach teenagers to respect authority or to rebel against authority? If you have ever raised children, you know you certainly do not have to teach them to rebel! It seems to come naturally, and we practically expect teenagers to struggle through that rebellious stage as they attempt to find their own identities. These simple examples clearly show that we are not born with a strong, alive spirit in perfect communion with the Holy Spirit.

This truth does not mean babies who die are destined to spend eternity in hell or that a man who never hears the Good News of Jesus has no hope in eternity. The Bible also teaches that God is just and righteous, and He knows how to take care of these situations. Romans 5:13 teaches that "sin is not imputed when there is no law." Since it is God's law that brings knowledge of sin and directs us to Jesus, this must mean that sin is not counted against one who has no knowledge of sin or who has received no direction to Jesus (Rom. 7:7; Gal. 3:24). In these cases, each man's conscience becomes a law unto himself, accusing him or else excusing him (Rom. 2:12–16).

In simple terms, God knows how to deal with each person's soul according to the truth to which he or she has been exposed and the opportunities with which he or she has been presented.

> *The Scriptures tell us plainly that eternal life is a free gift of God, not of works.*
>
> ❦

In this matter, I ascribe to the statement of John Wesley who, when asked how God deals with men who die having never heard the Good News of Jesus, declared; "Let it mean what it will, it cannot mean that the Judge of all the world is unjust. No scripture can mean that God is not love, or that his mercy is not over all his works."[1]

The bigger question is: What about the rest of humanity that is born into this world with a dead spirit and under the curse of sin? What hope do we have? The answer is that we must be "born again," just as Jesus told Nicodemus: "Most assuredly, I say to you, unless one is born again, he cannot see the kingdom of God. . . . unless one is born of water and the Spirit, he cannot enter the kingdom of God. That which is born of flesh is flesh, and that which is born of the Spirit is spirit. Do not marvel that I said to you, 'You must be born again'" (John 3:3–7).

Paul confirms this truth in the letter to the Ephesians:

And you *He made alive* who were dead in trespasses and sins, in which you once walked according to the prince of the power of the air, the spirit who now works in the sons of disobedience, among whom also we all once conducted ourselves in the lusts of our flesh, fulfilling the desires of the flesh and of the mind, [i.e. of the body and soul] and *were by nature children of wrath*, just as the others. But God, who is rich in mercy, because of His great love with which He loved us, even when *we were dead in trespasses, made us alive together with Christ* . . . (Eph. 2:1–5 emphasis added).

The simple fact is that, due to the sinful nature of Adam, we are all born into this world separated from God. We all soon commit our own individual sinful acts and so stand accused and guilty before God on both counts. But we must understand the truth. We are not sinners because we committed acts of sin. We committed sinful acts because we are by nature sinners. This would be a hopeless state had God left us to our own devices. All of the man-made religions, philosophies, and belief systems have been our attempt to get back to God or, perhaps more accurately, following the lie of Satan to "become as gods."

The truth is we cannot save ourselves; we must have a Savior. There is one and only one being in the universe who is capable of birthing new life into our dead spirits: Jesus the

Christ. There is no other name given by which man might be saved (Acts 4:12). "The first man Adam became a living being; the last Adam [Jesus] became a life-giving spirit" (1 Cor. 15:45). Following the right rules, rituals, or traditions cannot give life to our dead spirits. No other belief system—not Buddhism, Hinduism, Islam, New Age, or any other—has the power to reconcile us to our Creator. The only One capable is He who said: "It is the Spirit who gives life; the flesh profits nothing. The words that I speak to you are spirit, and they are life" (John 6:63). Only He can bring us back to God, for He, and only He, is the Lord of all spirits (Heb. 12:9). Jesus alone defeated the grave and holds the keys of death (Rev. 1:18). It is totally futile to attempt to get back to God in any other way. The dead cannot raise themselves. Jesus said, "I am the way, the truth, and the life. No one comes to the Father except through Me" (John 14:6). We must be born of the Spirit!

How is this new life gained? The Scriptures tell us plainly that eternal life is a free gift of God, not of works (Eph. 2:8–9). We must believe that Jesus is the Son of God, confess Him as Lord, believe that God raised Him from the dead, repent of our sins and be baptized. Our act of faith then applies the work of Jesus on the cross to our hearts, removing the guilt of sin which was upon us, and seals us with His Holy Spirit of promise (Col. 2:13–14; Eph. 1:13). The application of this work of the cross occurs in an instant of time. We are transported from the kingdom of darkness into the kingdom of light. We have entered the Kingdom of God and been born of the Spirit!

Questions for Reflection

1. What are the three main parts of man?

2. What is the body of man?

3. What is the soul of man?

4. What is the spirit of man?

5. What part(s) of man will live forever?

6. What was the lie spoken of in the Garden of Eden? What damage did it do?

7. Give some examples of evidence of a "dead" spirit within our nature.

8. How can we be born of the Spirit?

9. What change does this bring about?

10. Why can salvation be found in no one except Jesus?

11. Why can no other belief system or religion reconcile man to God?

✣ Chapter 4 ✣
Baptized with the Spirit

Once we have received the new birth of the Spirit, we are children of God and destined to spend eternity with Him. Were we to die at that time, our souls would be ushered into the presence of God in Heaven. But most of us live for some time on earth after our conversion. God designed it that way on purpose. Those who are alive in the Spirit are used by Him to spread the gospel of Jesus to those who are lost. Those alive in the Spirit are only "born of the Spirit"; we are just babes. In the natural realm, newborn babies are weak and almost powerless; so it is in the spiritual. We must grow in order to fulfill the designs of God for our lives. We must grow in order to be useful in the Kingdom of God. We are encouraged ". . . as newborn babes, desire the pure milk of the word, that [we] may grow thereby" (1 Pet. 2:2).

How do we grow? How do we get strength to carry out the will of God? To begin to answer these questions, let's look at three passages of "the pure milk of the word." Just prior to His ascension, the resurrected Christ instructed His disciples with these words: "Behold, I send the Promise of My Father upon you; but tarry in the city of Jerusalem until you are endued with power from on high" (Luke 24:49). The parallel passage from Acts 1:4–8 states it this way:

And being assembled together with them, He commanded them not to depart from Jerusalem, but to wait for the Promise of the Father, "which," He said, "you have heard from Me; for John truly baptized with water, but you shall be baptized with the Holy Spirit not many days from now. . . . But you shall receive power when the Holy Spirit has come upon you; and you shall be witnesses to Me in Jerusalem, and in all Judea and Samaria, and to the end of the earth."

The third passage is from the gospel of John 1:11–12: "He came unto his own, and his own received him not. But as many as received him, to them gave he power to become the sons of God, even to them that believe on his name" (KJV). Power is a common theme throughout these passages: ". . . endued with power . . . receive power . . . power to become . . . *power to become the sons of God.*" The power of God's Word helps us grow as Christians as well as carry out the will of God.

Imagine the effect these words must have had on those first disciples. These men had followed Jesus for three years. They had left their homes and families to travel with Him and put their careers on hold. They had seen Jesus perform many miracles; healing the sick, restoring sight to the blind, resurrecting the dead, calming the storm, walking on water, and casting out demons. The disciples had even been anointed by Jesus with the spiritual power to perform many of these same miracles (Luke 9:1–2, 10:17).

They had seen Jesus beaten, crucified, and buried; they had now seen this same Jesus resurrected from the dead. They had seen the once fatal wounds rendered harmless to His glorified body and were firsthand witnesses to His victory over death. They had received the new birth of the Spirit forty days before and had sat at the feet of this glorified, resurrected Christ off and on for forty days, being taught by Him concerning the wonders of the Kingdom of God.

If I were in their place, I know that I would feel prepared to go and do whatever God called me to do. I would be excited and ready to go! I would feel as if I had the knowledge (Jesus Himself was my teacher), the experience (over three years with Jesus and an eyewitness to the Resurrection), and the will to do whatever I was called upon to do. Have you thought about how you would react? I imagine some of these same thoughts went through the minds of the disciples as Jesus instructed them to wait in Jerusalem and wait for the power of the Holy Spirit.

Jesus knew that regardless of their preparation and the strength of their own wills, the disciples would fail if they attempted to live this new life in their own strength. It simply cannot be done. It is not a matter of strength of will or desire. It is not a matter of being too weak in the flesh. It is a matter of being strong enough in the Spirit. The disciples were literally stuck between Easter and Pentecost. They only stayed there for a few days. Sadly, today, many Christians spend almost their entire lives stuck between Easter and Pentecost and lack the strength of the Spirit.

Jesus promised them power after they received the baptism of the Holy Spirit. What was the purpose of this power they were to receive? This power enabled them to be witnesses to Jesus; witnesses to the facts that Jesus was indeed the only begotten Son of God, that He died, was buried, was resurrected, and that He ascended into heaven to the right hand of the Father. I often misinterpreted the passage: "you shall be witnesses to Me. . . ." (Acts 1:8) to mean "you shall go out and witness for Me." However, this is not what the passage says. It claims that we will *be witnesses* when the Holy Spirit has come upon us.

The emphasis is not so much on what we might say to others but in who we will become. In other words, when we have received the power of the Holy Spirit, our lives will be changed into lives that will be witnesses to the gospel of Christ simply by the way we live our lives. We will be new creatures: changed from the old and different from how we were before. That difference will be evident in our homes, workplaces, schools, and anywhere else we go about the activities of living. Paul told the Spirit-filled believers in Corinth that they were ". . . an epistle of Christ, ministered by us, written not with ink, but with the Spirit of the living God, not on tablets of stone but on tablets of flesh, that is, of the heart" (2 Cor. 2:3). One of my favorite quotations concerns this truth and is from St. Francis of Assisi: "Preach the gospel at all times; if necessary, use words."[1]

We can rest confidently in the truth that God will empower us to do whatever He calls us to do.

To understand and accept this simple truth of the gospel is incredibly liberating. Our acceptance by God and our effectiveness in His kingdom are no longer based upon our own abilities. This realization puts the power and responsibility where it rightfully belongs: in the power of God Himself.

This does not mean that we can neglect our duty. We cannot be lazy, undisciplined believers and still fulfill our calling. However, we can rest confidently in the truth that God will empower us to do whatever He calls us to do. Our effectiveness in His kingdom is not limited by our personal weaknesses and limitations, but by the degree of our dependence upon Him. The more dependent we are upon God, the more effective we will be and the more powerful we will be in the Spirit. We are instructed to, "Trust in the Lord with all your heart, and lean not on your own understanding; in all your ways acknowledge Him, and He shall direct your paths" (Prov. 3:3–6). This dependence upon God also provides protection against the common pitfall of pride in our own spirituality. Paul emphasizes the need to remember to Whom we owe honor and glory: ". . . we have this treasure in earthen vessels, that the excellence of the power may be of God and not of us" (2 Cor. 4:7).

What then does it mean to be baptized with the Holy Spirit? To be baptized means "to make overwhelmed."[2] When we are baptized with the Spirit, we no longer keep Him confined to our spirits. We receive Him into all of our being—all of who we are—spirit, soul, and body. We no longer only want His presence in our innermost sanctuary, but we desire His presence in every aspect of our lives. We not only desire the new birth which He bestows, but we also come to see our great need for His ever-present strength and guidance. We are no longer content to have our place in heaven secured, but we desire to be changed into the likeness of Jesus. We have caught some glimpse of the depth of our depravity and of the glory and majesty of our Lord. We desire Jesus to be our Lord and Savior. We begin to live the reality of John 7:38 that, ". . . out of his heart will flow rivers of living water."

To be baptized in the Spirit does not mean that we receive all of Him, but that He receives all of us. In baptism by immersion, the water contains all of you as you yield yourself to it. So it is with Spirit baptism. You do not contain all of the Spirit, but you yield yourself completely to Him. Only Jesus contained the complete fullness of the Holy Spirit (John 3:34; Col. 2:9). You have in essence invited Him to assume a predominant and profound influence over all of your thoughts, desires, goals, and actions.

Holy Spirit baptism does not bring about instant perfection of your soul. This requires a lifetime of walking in the Spirit, which we will discuss in the next chapter. Spirit baptism does not make your opinion always right or your interpretation of Scripture infallible. It does not mean that you are now better than any other Christians who haven't experienced God in this way or that you have arrived at some elite plane of spirituality.

It simply means that you have now received the power by which you may grow into spiritual maturity. Your life is no longer about trying to follow all the right rituals and rules, but about honoring your Heavenly Father who loves you and gave His only Son for you. His love has now been poured forth into your heart by His Spirit. It is this Spirit that now bears witness to your spirit that you are His child, and you receive the assurance of your salvation that will root and ground your soul (Rom. 5:5, 8:16). The Holy Spirit also implants within you a passion for God's Word and a strong desire for Jesus. You have received the power that allows your mind to be transformed and the desires of your heart to be changed. You have received the power to overcome your own sinful tendencies. You have received the *"power to become."*

Who baptizes you with the Holy Spirit? The answer is given by John the Baptist when he said, "I indeed baptize you with water unto repentance, but He who is coming after me is mightier than I, whose sandals I am not worthy to carry. He will baptize you with the Holy Spirit and with fire" (Matt. 3:11). He was speaking, of course, of Jesus. Peter confirmed this on the day of Pentecost. When asked to explain what was happening as those newly-Spirit-filled believers poured out into the streets of Jerusalem, Peter replied, "This Jesus God has raised up, of which we are all witnesses. Therefore being exalted to the right hand of God, and having received from the Father the promise of the Holy Spirit, He poured out this which you now see and hear" (Acts 2:32–33).

Jesus, and *only* Jesus, baptizes His followers with His Spirit. It is scriptural and proper that those in positions of spiritual leadership should lay hands on and pray for believers to be filled with the Holy Spirit. We see this pattern repeatedly in

Scripture. However, we must never mistakenly think that the power of the Spirit is bestowed by fellow men. The Promise of the Father, the Holy Spirit, is given only and directly by the Son.

But exactly how do you receive the Holy Spirit? This was a question that I wrestled with for some time after coming to acknowledge my great personal need for the power of the indwelling Spirit. I read every book I could find on Holy Spirit baptism. Many of these books indicated that there were certain steps to be followed or certain rituals to be done in preparation for receiving the baptism of the Spirit. More often

Sometimes the best prayer for those who are beginning this journey of life in the Spirit is simply to ask God to make them aware of their great need for Him.

than not, these books brought more frustration than peace to my soul. They seemed to imply that receiving this very vital gift was difficult.

This approach seemed contrary to the declaration of Peter on the day of Pentecost when he stated that "the promise is to you and to your children, and to all who are afar off, as many as the Lord our God will call" (Acts 2:38–39). I then began to see the simplicity of Scripture on this question. Luke 11:9–13 instructs, ". . . ask, and it will be given to you; seek, and you will find; knock, and it will be opened to you. For everyone who asks receives, and he who seeks finds, and to him who knocks it will be opened . . . how much more will your heavenly Father give the Holy Spirit to those who ask Him!" Paul wrote in Galatians 3:14 that we "receive the promise of the Spirit through faith." Just as I had received salvation as a young boy by simply asking Jesus into my heart and accepting what He had done for me, I could likewise receive the Holy Spirit by simply asking and believing. How simple! How profound! How just like God!

Furthermore, the Scriptures even instruct us how to ask for this blessing: "Blessed are those who hunger and thirst for righteousness, for they shall be filled" (Matt. 5:6); "'If anyone thirsts, let him come to Me and drink. He who believes in Me, as the Scripture has said, out of his heart will flow rivers of living water.' But this He spoke concerning the Spirit, whom those believing in Him would receive . . ." (John 7:37–39). Sincerely asking and seeking will be honored by God. Just as one who is dying of starvation longs for food, or one who is dying of thirst begs for water, so must be the desire of our heart for the Holy Spirit. True desire is born out of desperate need.

Sometimes the best prayer for those who are beginning this journey of life in the Spirit is simply to ask God to make them aware of their great need for Him. It is not difficult for one who is hungry to sit down to eat. It is not difficult for the child who has scraped his knee on the playground to seek comfort from his mother. But until the need becomes apparent, it is much easier to go on playing! If you are tired of playing at your faith, if you are tired of finding your beliefs incapable of transforming your life, if you have been wounded on the playground of life, then I encourage you to seek the Comforter of your Heavenly Father.

Questions for Reflection

1. What attitude must we embrace in order to be useful in the Kingdom of God?

2. Why were the disciples instructed to wait in Jerusalem for the promise of the Father?

3. Why was this next step so important for the disciples?

4. How can we receive "power to become the sons of God?" Why is this important for us?

5. What limits our effectiveness in His kingdom?

6. What does it mean to be baptized with the Spirit?

7. What effect does this baptism have on us?

8. Who baptizes us with the Holy Spirit?

9. How do we receive this baptism?

10. What is a sure sign that we have received this baptism?

11. One of the common points of discussion and disagreement about the baptism of the Holy Spirit concerns the gift of tongues. Some believers and some denominations consider the expression of tongues to be a necessary sign of a person's having received the baptism of the Holy Spirit. While this gift is often associated in Scripture with receiving the Spirit and is an important spiritual gift, it is never presented as a necessary outward sign of the inner change. After studying the following Scriptures, at what conclusion do you arrive?

Acts 2:1–4

Acts 4:8

Acts 6:1–6

Acts 8:14–17

Acts 10:44–46

Acts 19:1–7

1 Corinthians 12:4–11, 28–30

1 Corinthians 14:1–5

❧ *Chapter 5* ❧
Walking in the Spirit

I t should be obvious by now that life in the Holy Spirit is not about progressing through certain predictable stages or steps. Receiving the Holy Spirit is not a competition between the "haves" and the "have-nots" of the Christian faith. Rather, there exists a relationship between us as individual followers of Jesus Christ and His Spirit who dwells within us. This is an ever-deepening relationship, beginning at conversion, the depths of which will never be fully explored this side of heaven.

Scripture teaches that being filled with the Spirit is not a one-time experience but an ongoing state. "Do not be drunk with wine . . . but be filled with the Spirit . . ." (Eph. 5:18) means to be continually under the influence of the Holy Spirit. An analogy can be drawn to a sailboat upon the ocean. The boat may be launched and the sail be raised. The wind comes, fills the sail, and the boat begins to move. As long as the sail is trimmed to catch the wind, the boat continues to gain momentum and moves steadily along its chosen course. But should the sail be loosened and no longer turned to the wind, the boat slows and eventually stops moving.

The new birth could be likened to launching the boat, and Spirit baptism compared to hoisting the sail to catch that first gust that starts us moving. If we do not continue to be filled with the wind of the Spirit, however, we soon lose all momentum. If our sails are flat, we are no longer filled. The fact that we were once filled doesn't begin to address our present needs. Without the continual momentum provided by the wind, we slow down and begin to drift off course. This continual filling of the Spirit is referred to in Scripture as both walking in the Spirit and *being led by the Spirit*: "Walk in the Spirit, and you shall not fulfill the lusts of the flesh . . . [I]f you are led by the Spirit, you are not under the law" (Gal. 5:16, 18).

Walking in the Spirit means to live each day in an intimate, vital relationship with your Heavenly Father through the power and presence of the Holy Spirit. We are to live the reality of the New Covenant in Christ, knowing and relying upon the Spirit as helper, counselor, teacher, and friend. It means to be led by that Spirit into ministry in His gifts: teaching, prayer, compassion, healings, and discernment, among others. Please understand that the Spirit does not intend to make preachers out of all of us, but He does intend to make true disciples (followers) of Christ out of each of us. He needs laymen in the homes and workplaces to be witnesses in all walks of life.

The Epistles of the New Testament mainly address this aspect of Christian living. After the book of Acts, little is written about initial salvation or justification. Neither is there much instruction regarding the initial baptism of the Holy Spirit. Why? The writers were addressing born-again, Spirit-filled believers. Practically everyone in the churches to whom these Epistles were addressed had already been "saved" and "filled" because that was the norm; that is what was expected. The early church would never have allowed someone to come to believing faith in Jesus and failed to instruct them on the need of receiving the power of the Holy Spirit! Most of the instruction from the writers of the New Testament, therefore, concerned how to live daily in that relationship.

There are three main obstacles to living the type of Christian life to which we are called. These are sin, Satan, and self. The power of sin over us has been removed if we are in Christ. "Likewise reckon yourselves to be dead indeed to sin, but alive to God in Christ Jesus our Lord. Therefore do not let sin reign in your mortal body, that you should obey it in its lusts. . . . For sin shall not have dominion over you, for you are not under law but under grace" (Rom. 6:15). ". . . God was in Christ reconciling the world to Himself, not imputing their trespasses to them . . ." (2 Cor. 5:19). Our sins have been forgiven through the vicarious work of Christ on the cross, and they no longer have the power to separate us from God. In other words, Jesus took my sin to the cross and paid the required price—death of a perfect sacrifice. He did for me what I could not do for myself, as confirmed by this passage: "And you, being dead in your trespasses and the uncircumcision of your flesh, He has made alive together with Him, having forgiven you all trespasses, having wiped out the handwriting of requirements that was against us, which was contrary to us. And He has taken it out of the way, having nailed it to the cross" (Col. 2:13–14).

Satan has also been defeated and no longer has any power to keep a believer from totally living a Spirit-filled life. While it is true that he is still a strong and formidable adversary, the One who lives in us is stronger; ". . . He who is in you is greater than he who is in the world" (1 John 4:4). God allows Satan to accuse us and to tempt us in order to strengthen our faith. Satan cannot, however, remove us from the security and love of God. Satan cannot force us to do anything. He can only tempt and entice us. Jesus openly defeated Satan on the cross and by His victory over death. "Having disarmed principalities and powers, He made a public spectacle of them, triumphing over them in it" (Col. 2:15). By the simple act of faith, this victory over sin and Satan is instantly appropriated to the life of a believer at the time of conversion. The accomplishment of this victory is totally dependent upon the perfect and completed work of Christ.

What about self, the third enemy of a Spirit-filled life? Jesus also defeated the flesh or the old selfish nature on the cross. As the complete and perfect representative of mankind, He poured out His body and His soul as a sacrifice for sin (Isa. 53:5, 10, 12). He commended His spirit to His Heavenly Father (Luke 23:46). This work of the cross is sometimes referred to as the cocrucifixion. In the same sense that we were all "in Adam" when he sinned, so were we all "in Christ" on the cross.

> *The battle between the old nature and the new doesn't go away with the coming of the Holy Spirit.*

When we are baptized into His death, we kill the old self, that old sinful and fallen nature, "knowing this, that our old man was crucified with Him, that the body of sin might be done away with, that we should no longer be slaves of sin" (Rom. 6:6). Paul related this truth by saying, "I have been crucified with Christ; it is no longer I who live, but Christ lives in me; and the life which I now live in the flesh I live by faith in the Son of God, who loved me and gave Himself for me" (Gal. 2:20). These passages and others tell us that the old self does not have the power to prevent us from walking in the Spirit. The defeat of the sinful nature was accomplished by Jesus at Calvary.

That all sounds well and good, and I absolutely believe it to be true. But if you have been a Spirit-filled Christian for longer than a few minutes, you know that the battle between the old nature and the new doesn't go away with the coming of the

Holy Spirit. Actually, the battle intensifies the more you try to walk in the Spirit. Your old nature, your self-centered soul, was in control of your life up until the time you received the Spirit, and it doesn't relinquish control easily. Galatians 5:16–25 defines the battle very well:

> I say then; Walk in the Spirit, and you shall not fulfill the lust of the flesh. For the flesh lusts against the Spirit and the Spirit against the flesh; and these are contrary to one another, so that you do not do the things that you wish. But if you are led by the Spirit, you are not under the law. Now the works of the flesh are evident, which are: adultery, fornication, uncleanness, lewdness, idolatry, sorcery, hatred, contentions, jealousies, outbursts of wrath, selfish ambitions, dissensions, heresies, envy, murders, drunkenness, revelries, and the like; of which I tell you beforehand, just as I also told you in time past, that those who practice such things will not inherit the kingdom of God. But the fruit of the Spirit is love, joy, peace, longsuffering, kindness, goodness, faithfulness, gentleness, self-control. Against such there is no law. And those who are Christ's have crucified the flesh with its passions and desires. If we live in the Spirit, let us also walk in the Spirit.

Even though the power of the old nature has been defeated and cannot keep us from walking in the Spirit, we must choose daily to walk in the Spirit as the means to victory over the flesh. It is the daily act of choosing, the daily submitting of your will to God's, that brings victory over self. Jesus told us, "If anyone desires to come after Me, let him deny himself, and take up his cross daily, and follow Me" (Luke 9:23).

The cross Jesus asks us to carry is not a burden to bear, but a place to die to self. This work of the cross takes a lifetime to appropriate to our lives. Another way to consider this is simply that God sends us the Holy Spirit to give us the power to say "no" to ourselves!

Every day, many times, we have the opportunity to engage this enemy of self. Any time we are tempted to gossip, cheat, or lie, we are being tested. Any time we have the chance to do good for someone and expect nothing in return, we have an opportunity to defeat our selfish nature. Any time we graciously extend forgiveness to someone who has wronged us, we are victorious over the old nature. Each and every chance to sin is an equal chance to win! By choosing to walk in the Spirit at each turn of events, we are refusing to fulfill the lusts of the flesh.

The Scriptures help us to better understand this battle between the old and new natures.

> There is therefore now no condemnation to those who are in Christ Jesus, who do not walk according to the flesh, but according to the Spirit. For the law of the Spirit of life in Christ Jesus has made me free from the law of sin and death. For what the law could not do in that it was weak through the flesh, God did by sending His own Son in the likeness of sinful flesh, on account of sin: He condemned sin in the flesh that the righteous requirement of the law might be fulfilled in us who do not walk according to the flesh but according to the Spirit. . . . Therefore, brethren, we are debtors—not to the flesh, to live according to the flesh. For if you live according to the flesh you will die; but if by the Spirit you put to death the deeds of the body, you will live (Rom. 8:1–5, 12–13).

Notice that this promise of "no condemnation" is given to those who walk in the Spirit; not to those who are only born of the Spirit or even to those just baptized with the Spirit. If we, as Spirit-filled believers, choose to follow the tendencies of the old nature, we are not walking in the Spirit and, therefore, we bring condemnation upon ourselves. We suffer loss of intimacy with God, become rebellious and bitter, and we suffer the heavy hand of conviction. However, when we choose to give up our rights, when we no longer insist on our own way and follow

instead after the things of God, we walk in that wonderf
of "no condemnation" and participate in the righte
peace, and joy of the Holy Spirit.

The New Testament divides believers into two categories:
carnal and spiritual. "Carnal" is not a word that we use
frequently in conversation these days, but it simply means
natural, worldly, or fleshly. Notice that these categories are not
distinguishing believers from nonbelievers. Both carnal and spiritual groupings are referring to born-again followers of Jesus.

Paul wrote to the church at Corinth that, sadly, he "could
not speak to [them] as to spiritual people but as to carnal, as to
babes in Christ. I fed you with milk and not with solid food; for
until now you were not able to receive it, and even now you are
still not able; for you are still carnal. For where there are envy,
strife, and divisions among you, are you not carnal and
behaving like mere men?" (1 Cor. 3:1–3). Keep in mind, Paul is
writing to the *church* at Corinth, not some pagan social club!

These are people born of the Spirit, baptized in the Spirit,
and operating in the gifts of the Spirit. Why are they considered carnal believers? Paul knows they are still walking after
their old natures because
they are quarreling and
bickering among them-
selves; each of them is
demanding his own way
and is convinced that his
understanding of the
gospel is the only correct
one (1 Cor. 1:10–13,
3:4–5, 4:6–7, 5:1–2, 6:1).

> *The more dependent we are upon God, the stronger we are in the Spirit and the more effective we are in His kingdom.*

It is expected that new Christians will be carnal most of the
time early in their new life of faith. It is not expected that they
will remain that way for a long period of time.

The Holy Spirit provides us with daily opportunities to die to ourselves and live to God; to submit our will to His. Each time we choose wisely, we walk in the Spirit. Each time we insist on our own way, we walk in the flesh. The truth is that all of us who are Spirit-filled walk at times in the flesh and at times in the Spirit. As time passes, we should take advantage of the opportunities provided by the Spirit to grow and gradually walk more of the time in the Spirit and less in the flesh. Everyday problems, accidents, conflicts, and other life events are perfect opportunities that challenge our spiritual growth. Watchman Nee said it this way. "The Bible does not expect new Christians to be spiritual instantaneously; if they should remain as babes after many years, however, then their situation is indeed most pitiful."[1] He further teaches that:

> it ought to be viewed as very abnormal should a born-again Christian remain long in the flesh, fail to subdue the power of sin and live a life of ups and downs. A believer ought to allow the Holy Spirit to examine his heart and enlighten him as to what is prohibited by the law of the Holy Spirit and the law of nature, as to what hinders him from gaining temperance and self-control, and as to what rules him and deprives him of liberty in his spirit to serve God freely. Unless these sins are taken away, he cannot enter richly into spiritual life.[2]

There is a catch to all of this, of course. We don't have the strength to do it alone! We cannot, in our own power, deny ourselves. We may succeed in conquering one selfish stronghold or habit, only to have it replaced by another. That's why we must have the indwelling power of the Holy Spirit. He gives us the power to say "no" to ourselves and then fills that part of us with godly characteristics.

Once we have made that choice, we must lean totally upon the mercy and strength of God to perform in us that which we have just willed to do. Remember, the more dependent we are upon God, the stronger we are in the Spirit and the more effective we are in His kingdom. "Now to Him who is able to do exceedingly abundantly above all that we ask or think, according to the power that works in us, to Him be glory in the church by Christ Jesus to all genera-tions, forever and ever. Amen" (Eph. 3:20–21).

> *How do you know if you are walking in the Spirit or not?*

❌

This understanding of the process of spiritual maturity allows us to look at trials and temptations in a whole new way. The Bible instructs us, ". . . count it all joy when you fall into various trials . . ." (James 1:2). For a long time, I could understand rejoicing *in spite of* trials, but I had a really hard time understanding how to rejoice *because of* trials. Now I see. When I am tempted in some way to yield to my·old nature, whether it is lust, greed, anger, unforgiveness, or selfish ambi-tion, that is God's way of shining a spotlight into the dark recesses of my soul and exposing the strength of the old nature that still remains. If that tendency did not still have a foothold in me, I would no longer be tempted in that way. If my heart's desire is to be changed into the image of Christ, then I can rejoice with a glad heart at the revelation! My heart can joyfully cry out, "Thank you, God, for exposing the strength of sin that remains within me. I choose not to yield to the old way. Please, God, honor me and bless me with the strength of Your Comforter and my Helper and enable me to be victorious over this temptation!" I claim Paul's words: "Rejoice in the Lord always. Again I will say, rejoice!" (Phil. 4:4).

How do you know if you are walking in the Spirit or not? If your life is more characterized by depression than by joy, you are not *walking* in the Spirit. If your life is more described by confusion than peace, you are not being *led* by the Spirit. If your actions (and reactions) are more often worldly than righteous, *you are not Spirit-filled*. If your desires and goals are more self-centered than centered on the good of others, you are not *walking* daily with the One who gave His life for all. If you don't spend time daily with the One you profess as Lord, then *you are living a lie*. Ask the One who knows all things to reveal to you the intentions and desires of your own heart. "Walk in the Spirit, and you shall not fulfill the lusts of the flesh!" (Gal. 5:16).

Questions for Reflection

1. Is being filled with the Spirit a one-time experience? Why or why not?

2. What does it mean to "walk in the Spirit?"

3. What are three main obstacles to living the type of Christian life to which we are called?

4. Has the power of sin over us been removed? How?

5. Does Satan hold the power to defeat us?

6. How can we live in victory over sin and Satan?

7. What about the power of self? Can this also be defeated? How?

8. What must we do daily in order to walk in the Spirit?

9. What are the consequences of choosing to walk in the Spirit? Of choosing not to?

10. What is meant by a "carnal" believer?

11. How often must we "choose" to die to self?

12. When are we considered "spiritual" believers?

13. Do we have the power or strength to walk daily in the Spirit?

14. How can we "count it all joy" during times of trial?

15. How do we know if we are truly walking in the Spirit?

Chapter 6

The Spirit of Adoption

I want to explore this concept of walking in the Spirit from another vantage that emphasizes the great need for believers to grow into spiritual maturity. The initial blessing of the New Covenant is justification, otherwise known as forgiveness of sin and reconciliation to God. The second blessing, as previously discussed, is the baptism of the Holy Spirit, including the inner witness of Spirit to spirit giving us the assurance of our salvation. The highest blessing of the New Covenant is to be found in the meaning of the "Spirit of adoption." J. I. Packer, in his classic book *Knowing God*, says the main point about the biblical doctrine of adoption "is that it is the highest privilege that the gospel offers: higher even than justification."[1] Paul, in the letter to the church at Rome, said this: "For you did not receive the spirit of bondage again to fear, but you received the Spirit of adoption by whom we cry out, 'Abba, Father'" (Rom. 8:15).

The best explanation of this truth came from Fuchsia Pickett.[2] The general idea is that the ancient Middle Eastern practice of adoption was quite different from ours today in the Western world. Today, we might find a child who has no home and go through the legal process to make that child our own with all of the legal rights and privileges of our natural born children. That is not a bad analogy of what God does for us today when He brings us out of the kingdom of Satan and gives us a new name with all the rights and privileges of His kingdom. However, in the ancient Middle East, adoption meant something quite different.

When a baby boy was born into a family, he would be called their baby, their child, or their boy; later perhaps he would even be referred to as their young man. But the word "son" was never used to describe that child's relationship in the family. "Son" was a special title to be bestowed upon him at the appropriate time. Only after that child had grown, studied the family business, and proven capable of responsibility in the business and family name was this title given. Often, he would be well into his teenage years, or possibly even in his twenties with a family of his own, before this time would come. The time was determined by the father. When the father deemed that the boy was now worthy, he would call for a celebration—a feast—for the community. The father would gladly present the young man to the community with words to this effect: "Today, this boy has become my son. He has studied. He has grown. He is responsible. He is ready. I am proud of him." There would be great celebration at the "adoption" which had taken place. The father had now bestowed all rights, privileges, authority, and responsibility to his son.

> *For as many as are led by the Spirit of God, these are the sons of God.*
>
>

This idea of adoption clearly fits with Scripture. On the eve of His public ministry, at His baptism by John the Baptist, as Jesus is being presented before Israel formally for the first time, the Father speaks from heaven: "You are my beloved Son; in You I am well pleased" (Luke 3:22). Isaiah had prophesied long before, "For unto us a Child is born, unto us a Son is given; and the government will be upon His shoulder" (Isa. 9:6). The most significant name bestowed upon Jesus is Son of God. The author of the book of Hebrews explains this very well:

> God . . . has in these last days spoken to us by His Son, whom He has appointed heir of all things, through whom also He made the worlds; who being the brightness of His glory and the express image of His person, and upholding all things by the word of His power, when He had by Himself purged our sins, sat down at the right hand of the Majesty on high, having become so much better than the angels, as *He has by inheritance obtained a more excellent name than they. For to which of the angels did He ever say: "You are My Son, Today I have begotten You"? And again: "I will be to Him a Father, and He shall be to Me a Son"?* (Heb. 1:1–5 emphasis added).

As a child, Jesus "grew and became strong in spirit, filled with wisdom" (Luke 2:40). At the age of thirty He was ready to begin His ministry, and the Father invested full authority in Him (John 5:22–27).[3] The marvelous truth is that, through Jesus, the only begotten Son, we can all become sons of God— children of God who have grown and matured in wisdom and in spirit and can be entrusted with responsibility and authority in His kingdom. The following Scriptures make this very clear:

> But as many as received him, to them gave he power to become the sons of God . . . (John 1:12 KJV).

> But we see Jesus, who was made a little lower than the angels, for the suffering of death crowned with glory and honor, that He, by the grace of God, might taste death for everyone. For it was fitting for Him, for whom are all things and by whom are all things, in bringing many sons to glory, to make the captain of their salvation perfect through sufferings. For both

He who sanctifies and those who are being sanctified are all of one, for which reason He is not ashamed to call them brethren (Heb. 2:9–11).

Behold, what manner of love the Father hath bestowed upon us, that we should be called the sons of God. . . . Beloved, now are we the sons of God, and it doth not yet appear what we shall be: but we know that, when he shall appear, we shall be like him; for we shall see him as he is (1 John 3:1–2 KJV).

The Scriptures also clearly identify those among the children of God who become the sons of God. Romans 8:12–15 states, "Therefore, brethren, we are debtors—not to the flesh, to live according to the flesh. For if you live according to the flesh you will die; but if by the Spirit you put to death the deeds of the body, you will live. *For as many as are led by the Spirit of God, these are the sons of God.* For you did not receive the spirit of bondage again to fear, but you received the Spirit of adoption by whom we cry out, 'Abba, Father'" (emphasis added).

Remember, this passage was written to those who already believed in Jesus. Who does Paul identify as the sons of God and, therefore, entrusted with the authority and responsibility of God's kingdom? Not those who have only been born of the Spirit. Not even those who have only been baptized with the Spirit. The ones identified as the sons of God are those who have grown and matured,

> *There is a desperate need in the Body of Christ today for believers who have matured and are truly being led by the Spirit.*
>
> ✕

who exercise the choice of their will to follow after the things of the Spirit and refuse to give in to the old nature—those who are led by the Spirit. The author of Hebrews referred to these when he wrote: "But solid food belongs to those who are of full age [i.e., mature], that is, those who by reason of use have their senses exercised to discern both good and evil" (Heb. 5:14). These believers are no longer carnal but have become spiritual, and are given responsibility in the Kingdom. "Brethren, if a man is overtaken in any trespass, *you who are spiritual* restore such a one in a spirit of gentleness, considering yourself lest you also be tempted. Bear one another's burdens, and so fulfill the law of Christ" (Gal. 6:1 emphasis added).

There is a desperate need in the body of Christ today for believers who have matured and are truly being led by the Spirit. Only from that position can we see and understand clearly the will of God, allowing us to walk in the humility and spirit of servanthood exemplified by Christ.

The challenge we have before us as Spirit-filled believers is to grow and mature, to become responsible sons and daughters in the Kingdom of God. No organization functions well without responsible leadership: not a business, not a family, and certainly not the church. Leadership in the church is not limited to the clergy, but should involve spiritually mature laity properly exercising their spiritual gifts. The maturity required for spiritual leadership only comes from submission to the Lordship of Christ and a daily and continuous walk with His Spirit. We must hear the call of God today and receive the fullness of the Spirit of adoption!

Questions for Reflection

1. Describe the ancient Middle Eastern practice of adoption.

2. When was the title of "son" applied?

3. What change(s) did this adoption bring to the life of the son?

4. How does this correlate to our lives in Christ?

5. What is the significance of God's declaration at Jesus' baptism?

6. What significance does this hold for those who follow Jesus?

7. Do we need to be led by the Spirit today? Why or why not?

8. Where does maturity for spiritual leadership come from?

9. Why does the church need the leadership of spiritual believers who are willing recipients of the Spirit of adoption?

❧ Chapter 7 ❧
Being Full

Since the days of the Reformation, controversy has existed in the church over various manifestations of the Holy Spirit. Some have tried to lay claim to certain gifts or miracles as necessary visible evidences of the Spirit's presence. In Scripture, however, a number of truths are very clear concerning the characteristics of one who is truly filled with the Spirit. It is very helpful to concentrate on these central issues, and this focus certainly enables us to discern what evidences of the Spirit's influence are most important to God.

The first and most important evidence of being filled with the Holy Spirit is the presence of spiritual fruit in a person's life. Jesus said, ". . . by their fruits you will know them" (Matt. 7:20). As the identity of a tree is clearly made known by the fruit it bears, so is the heart of a person made visible by the spiritual fruit, or lack thereof, in his or her life. If the Spirit is active in a person's life and has been given His rightful place of influence in the heart and mind, He will produce fruit through that person. The fruit that the Spirit produces is the character of God, the personality of Christ. Paul lists this fruit of the Spirit in Galatians 5:22: ". . . the fruit of the Spirit is love, joy, peace, longsuffering, kindness, goodness, faithfulness, gentleness, self-control." Appropriately, this list begins with love. "God is love, and he who abides in love abides in God, and God in him" (1 John 4:16).

The one manifestation of the Spirit which is always present in one who is Spirit-filled is love: love for God, an assurance of God's love for him, and love for mankind. The character of God cannot be defined without this type of love, and neither can His Spirit be in control of a life without producing this type of fruit. The rest of the fruit of the Spirit is equally important. Notice that these are not separate fruits that develop independently of each other. They are all parts of a unified whole, like slices of an orange, and the fruit is incomplete if any slices are missing. They grow in us together as the Spirit transforms us. Robertson McQuilkin states it this way: "And Jesus never intended us to have a few little shriveled 'fruits,' just enough to prove we're alive and what kind of 'tree' we are. He promises a bumper crop—a lot of Jesus' characteristics. You might call it a 'full' crop."[1]

> *The one manifestation of the Spirit which is always present in one who is Spirit-filled is love.*
>
> ❧

Jesus promises that, if we abide in Him we will bear "much fruit" and that our joy will be full (John 15:5, 8, 11).

How can we be sure that the fruit of the Spirit is growing in our lives? This is a very important question because it is easy to deceive ourselves as to the degree of our spiritual maturity. To put it bluntly: most of us think we're better than we are. At the same time, there are individuals on the other end of the spectrum who can never see anything positive or good about what God is doing in their lives. Both viewpoints are wrong and harmful. Both extremes are used by Satan to hinder our spiritual growth and effectiveness in the Kingdom. So, how can we discern, objectively, if we are bearing true spiritual fruit? Again, I refer to Mr. McQuilkin:

There's one sure-fire way to know what your crop looks like. Do you have an accountability partner? Remember, Christlikeness is the one meaning of "full" only others know for sure. You need a fruit inspector! Here's a plan you may want to follow. Show your partner, or someone you can trust to be honest about it, the three lists of possible fruits . . . (Jesus' description of fruit, Paul's list, and the titles given the Spirit) and ask for an evaluation: "Is my life obviously full of any of these characteristics? Are there others you have to search for to find?"[2]

The operation of spiritual gifts in your life is another indication of being filled with the Spirit. We will discuss the gifts of the Spirit more thoroughly in chapter 9. For now, I would like to address a few general comments. Over twenty gifts of the Spirit are listed in the New Testament. These gifts cover all areas of ministry, including church organization, outreach ministries, preaching, teaching, healing, and deliverance. The simple fact is that if you are full of the Spirit, He will work through you in some of these gifts. The only way He will not work in you with spiritual gifts is if you refuse to let Him!

The manifestation of gifts in the life of a Spirit-filled believer is not some exceptional blessing of a select few, but is a necessary tool to do the will of God. There are no exceptions. No one is left out. God will use you if you make yourself available to be used. Don't get the idea that the gifts are just for church meetings and Sundays. They are to enable us to live everyday life in the power of the Spirit. They are to empower us to be witnesses. Some of the most wonderful manifestations of the Spirit's gifts which I have experienced have occurred during my daily routines when presented with an opportunity to talk with people about Jesus or to pray with them. You can tell that the Spirit is working through you in a supernatural[3] way because the results will be supernatural: the results will be better than what you could have expected had you been acting on your own.

Anointed teaching moves people closer to God with a desire for Him to transform their lives. *Anointed preaching* moves people to repentance and salvation. *Anointed compassion* touches people's hearts with the transforming and healing love of God. This has nothing to do with a person's eloquence or natural talents. We may marvel at the talent of a soloist in a worship service, but the Spirit may move more strongly in the anointed singing of one not so talented. You may feel awkward in sharing your faith in Christ with your next-door neighbor, but the Spirit takes the words of your mouth and uses them to implant a hunger for righteousness in the other's heart. Are spiritual gifts operating in your life? Look for the results, then give God the glory!

Another evidence of spiritual fullness is the blessing of God over your life. This isn't something you have to worry about or work for; it's just part of God's promise. We should never become preoccupied with seeking for God's blessings. We should instead be occupied with doing His will. God takes care of the blessings.

> *There are no exceptions. No one is left out. God will use you if you make yourself available to be used.*

He brings prosperity to us in ways that will not destroy us with the temptations of wealth. He brings health to us in ways that glorify Him. He watches over our children and creates peace in our homes. King David wrote: "Trust in the Lord, and do good: Dwell in the land, and feed on His faithfulness. Delight yourself also in the Lord, and He shall give you the desires of your heart. Commit your way to the Lord, Trust also in Him, and He shall bring it to pass. He shall bring forth your righteousness as the light, and your justice as the noonday" (Ps. 37:3–6).

The Lord promises us great blessings as we live with Him. It's critical, however, to set our priorities correctly. We shouldn't strive to "delight in the Lord" *for the purpose* of having our desires met. That narrow attitude feeds off the old self-centered nature. It smacks of a very worldly, "What's in it for me?" mentality. We should delight ourselves in the Lord because of who He is and all He represents. It is His job to then bless us as He sees fit. If we get this right, His heart's desires become our heart's desires.

Don't ever fall into the trap of looking at another's life from the outside and trying to judge his or her spiritual condition by the outward circumstances of his or her life. Bad things happen to good people and good things happen to bad people. The real blessings are on the inside, in the hidden regions of the soul. The real blessings can be seen in people's lives as they learn how to handle both prosperity and poverty with contentment, persevere through adversity, and come out on the other side with no bitterness but with hearts full of joy. Real blessing can be seen as people face death with confidence and assurance. The real blessing is peace that passes understanding, a peace that transcends the circumstances of our lives, a peace that cannot be shaken regardless of what life throws at us. Many are the blessings of God!

In summary, I ask, "What does it look like to be filled with the Holy Spirit?" It means that, from your personal perspective, you know the inner righteousness, peace, and joy that come from being submitted to Him (Rom. 14:17). As you spend time daily with the Spirit of wisdom, understanding, counsel, power, knowledge, and fear of the Lord, He transforms you (Isa. 11:2). Those attributes slowly become your own, and you know that you're different inside. You are more settled, and your life is no longer predominated by peaks and valleys. You are no longer so easily shaken by adversity, but when you are, you find it much easier to regain your balance. You find that your first conscious thoughts of the morning and your last ones in the evening are now focused on Jesus. You have a deep inner desire not to let any thought, word, or action bring dishonor to your Heavenly Father. Only you (and, of course, God) know for sure what you look like from this inner vantage point.

From an outside perspective, or how others see us, "full" looks like Jesus! As the fruit of the Spirit grows on the inside, some of it becomes visible from the outside. Jesus begins to use us to reach out to people around us through the gifts of His Spirit. Those who are around us can quickly tell if we're filled with the Holy Spirit. All they have to do is observe the way we live, work, interact with people, handle adversity, pursue entertainment, and the many other aspects of daily life. One of the absolute worst witnesses to Jesus are those who proclaim to be Spirit-filled, yet live most of their lives by the power of their old spiritless nature. Only others know for sure what you look like from outside. That's why we need the "fruit inspectors"!

These words from Paul's letter to the church at Ephesus remind us what it means to be full of the Spirit:

> For this reason I bow my knees to the Father of our Lord Jesus Christ, from whom the whole family in heaven and earth is named, that He would grant you, according to the riches of His glory, to be strengthened with might through His Spirit in the inner man, that Christ may dwell in your hearts through faith; that you, being rooted and grounded in love, may be able to comprehend with all the saints what is the width and length and depth and height—to know the love of Christ which passes knowledge; that you may be filled with all the fullness of God (Eph. 3:14–19).

Questions for Reflection

1. What are the fruits of the Spirit?

2. Why are they clear evidence of being filled with the Holy Spirit?

3. Why does the list of those fruits begin with love?

4. How can we be sure that the fruit of the Spirit is growing in our lives?

5. Why do we need "fruit inspectors" in our lives?

6. Name another indication of being filled with the Spirit.

7. What are the gifts of the Spirit and why are they given to those who walk in the Spirit?

8. Why are the blessings of God another evidence of spiritual fullness?

9. Why should we delight ourselves in the Lord?

10. What does it look like to be filled with the Holy Spirit?

❧ Chapter 8 ☙
The Rest of God

A wonderful teaching in the Scriptures starts in the very first part of Genesis, extends into the New Testament, and reveals a crucial characteristic of life lived in the fullness of the Spirit. This characteristic is one of "rest." God's rest does not refer to a state of inactivity but deals with the source of strength for our actions.

Referring to the rebellious and unfaithful generation of Hebrews who were delivered out of Egyptian bondage, the Psalmist wrote: "So I swore in My wrath, 'They shall not enter My rest'" (Ps. 95:11). He was referring to the fact that the older generation did not have faith in God to bring them safely into their new home after they received word of the giants and strong men who occupied the land (Num. 13–14). Thus, the Hebrews were kept wandering in the wilderness until that generation of adults died before God would allow the younger generation to enter the promised land of Canaan. This older generation repeatedly rebelled against the very God who had miraculously delivered them from bondage. Even though they had experienced the power of God firsthand, they could not fathom that God Himself would provide the strength they needed to do the work at hand. They had more fear of their enemies than they had faith in God.

The book of Hebrews picks up this theme with a New Testament application:

> And to whom did He swear that they would not enter His rest, but to those who did not obey? So we see that they could not enter in because of unbelief. Therefore, since a promise remains of entering His rest, let us fear lest any of you seem to have come short of it. For indeed the gospel was preached to us as well as to them; but the word which they heard did not profit them, not being mixed with faith in those who heard it. For we who have believed do enter that rest. . . . For He has spoken in a certain place of the seventh day in this way: "And God rested on the seventh day from all His works. . . ." There remains therefore a rest for the people of God. For he who has entered His rest has himself also ceased from his works as God did from His. Let us therefore be diligent to enter that rest . . . (Heb. 3:18–4:11).

The Scripture draws an analogy between the seventh day of creation, the entering of the Promised Land, and a place of rest to which we are beckoned today. Where's the similarity? God created for six days then rested on the seventh day. Does that mean that God kicked back in His heavenly recliner, turned on the football game, and did nothing? Of course not! On day six of creation, God made man and gave him these instructions: "Be fruitful and multiply; fill the earth and subdue it; have dominion over the fish of the sea, over the birds of the air, and over every living thing that moves on the earth" (Gen. 1:28).

In other words, God gave man everything he needed and then He put man in charge of the earth and the animals. God rested, but He continued to work with man, instructing him, advising him, sustaining him. But man was in charge of the earth and its fortunes, within certain bounds, were in his hands. When a believer enters the rest which God provides, he ceases "from his works as God did from His."

We enter into God's rest by turning ourselves back over to God and putting God in charge of our lives. The Israelites were provided with a land all prepared for their arrival, but they would not believe and trust in God's strength to obtain it. They would still have had to work the land and harvest the crops, but God promised them a prosperous land and a bounty of blessing. Yet they did not believe. They would not rest and allow God to be in charge.

Jesus taught this same truth in this way: "Come to Me, all you who labor and are heavy laden, and I will give you rest. Take My yoke upon you and learn from Me, for I am gentle and lowly in heart, and you will find rest for your souls. For My yoke is easy, and My burden is light" (Matt. 11:28–30). We put yoke on oxen so we can have some measure of control over them and accomplish productive work. Without the yoke as a means of control, a team of oxen will wander aimlessly at best and perhaps even become destructive.

> *We enter into God's rest by turning ourselves back over to God and putting God in charge of our lives.*

Likewise, Jesus encourages us to take His yoke and place it on ourselves. He will never force His yoke of control on us; that would violate His own principle of free will. But He knows what is best for us, so He asks us to willingly take on His yoke and put Him in control. He promises that we will find rest in doing this. For what does He promise rest? Not our bodies. Often when Jesus is in control of our lives, we are physically busier than ever before, for the needs of the kingdom are many. Not for our spirits, either. In fact, as we learn to walk more and more in the fullness of the Holy Spirit, our spirits grow and become stronger and once again assume the predominant place in our being that God intended. The more we are in active communication with the "Father of spirits" (Heb. 12:9), the more active is our spirit. He promises rest for our souls. But do we need rest for our souls?

Our souls are comprised primarily of our intellect, will, and emotions. When the soul is not properly submitted to the spirit, it tends toward the old nature, as discussed earlier. This tendency is *always* there and will *remain* as long as we are at home in this earthly body.

> *Full surrender to Jesus is the place of rest.*

When not willingly placed under the influence and sovereignty of Jesus, our souls tend to get us in lots of trouble.

Where do all of the strongholds of the flesh reside? In the soul! From where does our tendency for selfishness come? What about fear, greed, depression, hatred, sexual immorality, and any number of other sins and harmful vices? The answer for all is that these tendencies reside in our own, worldly-natured, self-centered, flesh-bound souls. This is why James tells us, "Let no one say when he is tempted, 'I am tempted by God,' for God cannot be tempted by evil, nor does He Himself tempt anyone. But each one is tempted when he is drawn away by his own desires and enticed" (James 1:13–14). He further asks us, "Where do wars and fights come from among you? Do they not come from your desires for pleasure that war in your members? You lust and do not have. You murder and covet and cannot obtain. You fight and war. Yet you do not have because you do not ask" (James 4:1).

What's the solution to this dilemma? Enter into the rest that God has prepared for all believers. Place God in control of your life. Yield yourself daily to His sovereignty. Don't believe

Satan's lie that you must maintain control of your life. The secret place of rest is found only in full submission to the Lordship of Jesus. Full surrender to Jesus *is* the place of rest.

Andrew Murray says it this way:

> A full surrender is to obey as well as to trust, to trust as well as to obey. . . . It is not the yoke, but resistance to the yoke, that makes the difficulty; the wholehearted surrender to Jesus, as at once our Master and our Keeper, finds and secures the rest.[1]

Trust Him, as He urges you to do, and He will defeat the giants in your life. Stand steadfast upon His Word and watch Satan flee! Enter into the rest of the Promised Land for your soul and enjoy life in the Spirit.

Questions for Reflection

1. What is meant by the "rest" of God?

2. What is one of the greatest hindrances to entering into His rest?

3. Why is disobedience a hindrance to entering into His rest?

4. Did God stop working on the seventh day of creation? Why or why not?

5. Why did Jesus encourage us to take His yoke upon ourselves?

6. Do we need rest for our souls?

7. What happens when our souls (intellect, will, and emotions) are not properly submitted to the Spirit?

8. Name some of the strongholds of the flesh. Where do they reside?

9. When are we tempted?

10. Where can we find the place of rest?

❧ Chapter 9 ❧
Gifts of the Spirit

In chapter seven, we touched briefly on the gifts of the Holy Spirit. Let's now look at this topic in greater detail. Few things have caused more controversy in churches than the gifts of the Spirit. In all seriousness, biblical teaching on the gifts has been sorely lacking in most mainline churches of the modern era. This is probably because most people say that teaching about spiritual gifts raises too many questions and people have a tendency to get out of order if you start focusing too much on these gifts. Others continue to argue that people get carried away with healings and tongues and the like and create all sorts of confusion in the church—and they would be right! Misplaced focus and confusion certainly occur without proper instruction that is held under God's proper authority. The church at Corinth was a perfect example.

All of the gifts of the Spirit were operating in the Corinthian church, and they were definitely causing lots of mayhem. What was Paul's solution? He did *not* tell them to immediately cease and desist in the spiritual gifts. He told them that he did not want them to be ignorant of the gifts or of their practical applications (1 Cor. 12:1). He instructed them that all things needed to be kept decent and orderly (1 Cor. 14:40). Paul proceeded to give them detailed instructions regarding the practice of spiritual gifts and the need for them to be used properly.

It is important to note that Paul *did not try to stop the expression or use of the gifts,* even though some problems had arisen from the exercise of those gifts. Paul correctly understood that the gifts of the Spirit are absolutely essential if we are truly to be the church: the body of Christ. If we do not allow for the free exercise of spiritual gifts, then we are just playing at being the church. The supernatural work of grace requires supernatural tools! Without the operation of the gifts, we have nothing to offer people except some historical and doctrinal truth and a philosophical belief system. Jesus is alive and well at the right hand of the Father, and He works today through the lives of His redeemed upon the Earth. The gifts of the Spirit are the tools He has provided to do the work that He needs done.

> *Paul correctly understood that the gifts of the Spirit are absolutely essential if we are truly to be the church.*
>
> ❧

These are the exact same tools Jesus used to minister to folks as He traveled around Galilee. The Father's work included not only telling the Good News but also manifesting the power of His Kingdom. If we could do the work today without the tools, He would not have provided them so abundantly. I imagine that Satan is very pleased when we respond to controversy regarding spiritual gifts by shutting them down. Without gifts such as discernment, words of wisdom, prophecy, and teaching in operation, Satan's work is certainly much easier!

From reading the previous paragraphs, you can probably discern how I feel about the gifts of the Holy Spirit. But you need to know how I arrived at this position. I grew up in very traditional United Methodist congregations in Tennessee. I had good preachers and good teachers over the years, but I heard almost nothing about the Holy Spirit and even less about His gifts.

When I was nine years old, after listening to a sermon with the theme that we never knew how much time we had left to respond to God's call, I accepted Jesus as my Savior. To the refrains of "Just as I Am," I walked forward and sincerely accepted Jesus into my heart. I was baptized, and my name entered the rolls of the church.

For several Sundays after, I felt a need to go forward at the end of the service for prayer. This was not common or even considered desirable in those days. So after two or three Sundays, my pastor told me not to come forward anymore and assured me that my salvation was secure. I didn't know then how to express what was in my heart. I didn't doubt my salvation, but I still felt like something was missing or incomplete. Only years later did I come to understand that my heart was yearning for the complete Christian baptism—not just in water, but in the Spirit also.

I knew lots of good people in the church over the years, but for the most part they really didn't seem to be any different from most of the other good people I knew who didn't go to church. We would go each Sunday and have a nice service and occasionally someone would get baptized, usually a young adult following a confirmation class. My parents were always great about reaching out to those in need and trying to be there to help people. I would catch glimpses of spiritual power in the transforming effects of their acts of kindness (I later came to realize that these were some of the spiritual gifts in operation). There were a few faithful saints in the church who had experienced the baptism of the Spirit during the preceding few years and had been interceding and teaching at every opportunity. Most notably, one of these was my former high school English teacher. She opened her home to our youth group while I was still in high school, and God used her and that setting to prepare both me and my future wife (and many others) to receive His Spirit of promise.

Then, in the spring of 1983, Jackie and I were contacted by a local Christian man whom we had previously known only by name. He wanted to sponsor us for a short course in Christianity known as the Walk to Emmaus. This program involves three days of study and sharing in a retreat format and is designed to strengthen and raise up spiritual leadership in the church. Men go through the program on a designated weekend and their spouses attend two weeks later. The guidelines strongly encourage that both spouses attend.

I was a bit reluctant to go, but Jackie really wanted to, so I agreed. We sent in our applications and were accepted for the Walk (both the men's and women's) in June of that year.

Previously, I have related some of the story regarding my personal search for a deeper relationship with God. Through a period of searching, my heart had been brought to that place of brokenness which is necessary to being ready to receive whatever God wants to bestow upon us. God used this time away from work and the daily routine to continue to answer my cries for "something more."

Late one evening during the Walk, I was sitting quietly in the front of the sanctuary with only two or three other men who were likewise in prayerful contemplation. My love for God was growing as was my appreciation for His grace in my life. I had been brought to the realization that without an ongoing and vital relationship with God, all of life's other endeavors are meaningless.

As I sat on the floor in that darkened sanctuary, the cross hanging upon the wall above me, God blessed me with the baptism of His Spirit. I felt the love of God pour down from the cross in a most palpable way. The best way I can describe the feeling would be "liquid love." This love poured into my heart until it felt like it would explode. It then began to erupt from deep within and flow outward until my entire being was engulfed. I knew I was changed. I had previously known God, but had never experienced His presence in such a personal and powerful way. That evening, God implanted a power within me, just as He had planted in those disciples gathered in the Upper Room long ago. I felt alive as never before! I had been touched by a love so powerful that everything else paled in comparison; a love that brought everything else into proper perspective.

Over the ensuing weeks, my passion for God continued to grow. I could not get enough of His Word. I could not spend enough time in prayer and worship expressing my love for Him. Three weeks after that special evening, while praying alone in my living room, I was telling God how much I loved Him and appreciated the work He was doing in my life and in Jackie's. I was praying aloud, but very quietly. After some time, I exhausted all the ways I knew of verbally expressing what was in my heart, but I was reluctant to leave the intimate time with my Father. So I continued to linger. I soon realized that I had continued to pray aloud, and was still expressing my love for Him, but with words which were unknown to my mind. The Spirit was aiding my prayers and my heart's desire to praise my Heavenly Father (Rom. 8:26). This was my personal introduction to one of the manifestations of the gift of tongues, which many refer to as a "prayer language" (1 Cor. 14:2). This gift has continued to be an active and important part of my spiritual walk since that time.

After receiving the baptism of the Spirit at the age of twenty-five, I realized that there was no power in most of our church services. We proclaimed to have the Word of Truth and the Bread of Life, but we acted more like the "frozen chosen." I realized that not only did I personally need something more in my life, but the church was also in desperate need of that same "something."

The words of Scripture began coming alive to me. I saw clearly that the lack of spiritual power in a church directly corresponded to the absence of spiritual gifts. We claimed the presence of Jesus with us, but we rejected by default the notion that He might want to do anything while we were gathered together. We seemed to be willing to accept the idea that God could influence the thoughts of our preachers and teachers, but that was about the extent of our collective desire for the things of the Spirit. This certainly didn't seem consistent with the gatherings of the early church recorded in the Acts of the Apostles. My heart began to cry out to God, "But what about the ministries of healing and deliverance? What about preaching and prophetic words that can set our hearts ablaze? What about worship that is empowered with Life itself? What about people who are hurting and in bondage?" Thus I came to see the need for the practical operation of spiritual gifts. I came to believe in them explicitly because the Bible said they were real and because the need for them had never gone away. I came to believe in the validity and reality of the gifts before I ever actually experienced them. I came to accept them on faith.

The following Scripture passages show us the gifts of the Holy Spirit:

> For as we have many members in one body, but all members do not have the same function, so we, being many, are one body in Christ, and individually members of one another. Having then gifts differing according to the grace that is given to us, let us use them: if prophecy, let us prophecy in proportion to our faith; or ministry, let us use it in our ministering; he who teaches, in teaching; he who exhorts, in exhortation; he who gives, with liberality; he who leads, with diligence; he who shows mercy, with cheerfulness (Rom. 12:4–8).

> Now concerning spiritual gifts, brethren, I do not want you to be ignorant. . . . There are diversities of gifts, but the same Spirit.

There are differences of ministries, but the same Lord. And there are diversities of activities, but it is the same God who works all in all. But the manifestation of the Spirit is given to each one for the profit of all: for to one is given the word of wisdom through the Spirit, to another the word of knowledge through the same Spirit, to another faith by the same Spirit, to another gifts of healings by the same Spirit, to another the working of miracles, to another prophecy, to another discerning of spirits, to another different kinds of tongues, to another the interpretation of tongues. But one and the same Spirit works all these things, distributing to each one individually as He wills. For as the body is one and has many members, but all the members of that one body, being many, are one body, so also is Christ. . . . Now you are the body of Christ, and members individually. And God has appointed these in the church; first apostles, second prophets, third teachers, after that miracles, then gifts of healings, helps, administrations, varieties of tongues. Are all apostles? Are all prophets? Are all teachers? Are all workers of miracles? Do all have gifts of healings? Do all speak with tongues? Do all interpret? But earnestly desire the best gifts" (1 Cor. 12:1, 4–12, 27–31).

But to each one of us grace was given according to the measure of Christ's gift. Therefore He says: "When He ascended on high, He led captivity captive, and gave gifts to men" . . . And He Himself gave some to be apostles, some prophets, some evangelists, and some pastors and teachers, for the equipping of the saints for the work of the ministry, for the edifying of the body of Christ, till we all come to the unity of the faith and of the knowledge of the Son of God, to a perfect man, to the measure of the stature of the fullness of Christ; that we should no longer be children, tossed to and fro and carried about with every wind of doctrine, by the trickery of men, in the cunning craftiness of deceitful plotting, but, speaking the truth in love, may grow up in all things into Him who is the head—Christ—from whom the whole body, joined and knit together by what every joint supplies, according to the effective working by which every part does its share, causes growth of the body for the edifying of itself in love (Eph. 4:7–8, 11–16).

Here is a summary of the gifts mentioned in the previous passages:

- Prophecy
- Service (ministry)
- Teaching
- Exhortation (encouragement)
- Giving
- Administration (ruling or government)
- Mercy (compassion)
- Word of Wisdom
- Word of Knowledge
- Faith
- Helps
- Gifts of Healings
- Working of Miracles
- Discernment of Spirits
- Tongues
- Interpretation of Tongues
- Apostle
- Prophet
- Evangelist
- Pastor
- Teacher

Most people from mainline churches have the tendency to look at this list and subconsciously begin separating the gifts into two main categories: 1) talents and natural abilities—things we're comfortable with—and 2) supernatural manifestations—things we're uncomfortable with. The only problem with this division is that the Bible makes no such distinction. The Bible just includes all gifts into one big package. They are all supernatural. There is no indication that we need some of these gifts more than others. As a matter of fact, Paul clearly makes the argument that all gifts are needed and that none should be excluded (1 Cor. 12:14–26).

Depending upon your background, there will almost certainly be some gifts that you are more comfortable with than others. You may have categorized some of the gifts with certain denominations or groups of Christians. You may have decided there are some of the gifts you consider okay and some that you never want to own. But, as you can see, this type of thinking is not consistent with biblical teaching.

We either need the gifts or we don't! If we need them, then what right do we have telling God which ones we'll accept and which ones we want Him to keep bottled up? Do we really think that God would provide something for our use that is harmful? If you are not comfortable with the idea of a church leader laying hands on someone and praying for healing, would you still be willing to have that done in your church if you knew that God would touch someone's life and heal him? If you are not comfortable with tongues, could you consider it just possible that through a message given in tongues, with interpretation, someone might be brought to repentance and turn his life over to Jesus?

If these things happened in your church, would the results be worth your discomfort? Would you have the sense not to reject the Spirit of Christ when He shows up to minister just because He doesn't do things exactly as you wanted Him to? Or would you be like the Pharisees in Jesus' time, who had become so wrapped up in the trappings of their religion that they could not recognize Jesus for who He is?

Might this change your church services a little? You bet! You're likely to have addicts and prostitutes coming up to your altar for prayer. You'll probably have those with cancer and other diseases coming forward openly seeking God's blessings of healing and power. You may occasionally have to quietly step across someone who has fallen under the power of the Spirit after receiving deliverance at the close of the service! Why, if you're not careful, it might look just like one of those Galilean hillsides long ago where Jesus was preaching. Or there might not be much outward manifestation at all as people pray for each other. Yet the Spirit may be ministering powerfully, healing and delivering. It is erroneous to think that anyone can judge what's happening inwardly by what is visible externally.

What right do we have telling God which gifts we'll accept and which ones we want Him to keep bottled up?

❧

This type of ministry has been active in my home church for the past fourteen years. I want to assure you that this ministry in the gifts of the Spirit can and does occur in decency and order. Unbelievably, when the manifestations of the Holy Spirit began occurring at the main Sunday morning worship service, nobody left! I don't just mean nobody left that particular service; I mean nobody left the church. With a church of over three hundred active members at the time, that's a miracle!

For fifteen years, I served as chairman of our church council, so if there had been much controversy over the services, I would have certainly known about it. Nobody left because everybody began to see the spiritual fruit that was produced. Bible studies started in homes or at church every day and night of the week. People who had come in off the street in search of Jesus found Him. Folks were being baptized every week. People were miraculously healed of cancer, heart disease, and many other illnesses and afflictions.

Those who were not physically healed were held and comforted by loving, compassionate brothers and sisters in Christ, and we came to see that death is not defeat: only death without Jesus is defeat. Hospital rooms were filled with friends praying. Many were delivered of demonic oppression. Members were getting together for prayer at all times of the day and night. Several members went on missionary trips. Our youth group tripled in size. Some members were called into full-time ministry. Our prayer chapel was always open and very commonly you could go there in the middle of the night and find someone in intercessory prayer.

It was not unusual for fifty or more people to come forward for ministry at the close of our services. The power of the Spirit would move so strongly at times that there might be twenty or more people lying prostrate on the floor. The district super-intendent (the pastor's pastor) once asked Tom Halliburton, our pastor at that time, how the older members of the congre-gation were doing with all the changes and spiritual manifestations. Tom replied, "I haven't asked them, but they seem to be okay with it. I have to step over them at the end of the service just like I do everyone else!"

The intensity of the outward manifestations of the Spirit has waxed and waned over the years. That's accepted and expected, because the needs are not always the same. Sometimes the Spirit works in quieter, but equally powerful ways. The point is this: how He works at any given time needs to be up to Him, not designated or limited by us.

It was during this time that the lessons upon which this book is based were developed. An acquaintance came to my office one day and asked me to teach a series on the Holy Spirit at his church. Since I had never done that, other than in the adult Sunday school class I taught, I told him I would pray about it. After prayerful consideration I felt directed to go, so we soon launched into an eight-week series on the person and work of the Holy Spirit. That was almost fourteen years ago, and God has blessed me with the opportunity to teach this course on the Spirit in many churches and many different settings.

From the beginning, He impressed upon me not to limit the lessons to just an intellectual exercise, but to allow people the freedom to experience the Holy Spirit personally. I have closed each series with a night of prayer ministry. Whenever possible, I will have a prayer team with me including, but not limited to, my wife and my pastor. God has blessed these times in such sweet and powerful ways.

I have been blessed to see Him minister to people just as He promises in His Word. I have witnessed the gifts of the Spirit in operation, both in myself and others, as God has reached out to meet the needs of people. I have witnessed the miraculous flow of words of knowledge, discernment, wisdom, healing, and prophecy all blended into a "holy whole" to set people free from their bondage to sin. I have seen people who have been oppressed for years leave these prayer times liberated; I've had the chance to stay in touch with many of these people throughout the years and have seen the fruit of the Spirit grow in their lives.

I have seen people fall down under the power of the Holy Spirit and rise up as new people with the confirmation of the inner change seen in their lives over the ensuing days, weeks, months, and years. God has blessed this hard-headed, skeptical, scientifically-trained man in more ways than I can possibly relate. At one time, I was as skeptical and doubting about these supernatural gifts as anyone. But my Heavenly Father touched me with the Finger of God, and I've never been the same, praise God!

There is a common error that people easily fall into regarding the exercise of spiritual gifts in worship services, and maybe this is a good place to address it. People (prayer intercessors and musicians seem especially prone to this tendency) start thinking that the gifts are what the service is all about. Almost imperceptibly and subconsciously they begin glorifying the gifts instead of the Giver! They expend all of their energy trying to recreate an experience or feeling they previously had. If we aren't careful, the time when the body is gathered together stops being about Jesus at all, and people leave disappointed if they didn't experience what they expected or didn't get their emotional fix. Avoiding this trap requires mature leadership and worship and prayer team members who desire to be submissive to authority and who truly have servant hearts.

The concept of the gifts of the Spirit is really quite simple. They are tools given to the church to do the work that God wants and needs done—no more and no less. If you can remember this simple definition, it may keep you from serious error. The gifts are not some sign of great spiritual maturity, and they are not badges of honor to be worn so that all can see.

Imagine a construction worker, checking in with his boss in the morning to get the day's assignment. He picks up his toolbox and heads out to the worksite. Upon arriving, he finds that someone has nailed up some two-by-fours across the doorway to the building and nobody can get in. He reaches in the toolbox and comes out with a saw. He then proceeds to cut off the boards to clear the way. Once the job is finished, what does he do with the saw? Does he hold it high in the air and walk around proclaiming to all the other workers how good he is with that saw? Of course not! He just drops the saw back in the box until such time as it might be needed again.

Not long after, he rounds a corner and finds a large nail sticking out at just the right height to catch an ear if someone isn't looking. He reaches in the toolbox, pulls out a hammer, and drives the nail in out of the way. What does he now do with the hammer? You guessed it. He quietly drops it back in the box; job completed. Step by step, the workers use the tools to build the house. This is a simple analogy, and hopefully the message is clear. The gifts are *tools*, not *merit badges*!

Tools are provided to workers. If you are willing and prepared to work in the Kingdom of God to help build His house (Eph. 2:19–22), He will provide you with all the tools you need. If you're content to sit around, drink coffee, eat donuts, watch others work, and talk about the fine house that's being built (or criticize the work), you don't need tools.

The Spirit chooses what gifts each and every individual is given. If we have a special yearning in our heart for a particular ministry, according to Scripture, it's okay to pray for that gift as long as we are willing to leave the final decision up to Him. Everyone who is willing to work will be given at least one gift. Nobody is left out. Likewise, nobody will be given all the gifts. The only individual to operate in all the spiritual gifts is Jesus.

I believe it is consistent with scriptural teaching and example that any believer may operate in many different gifts during their lifetime, depending upon the need of the moment and the responsibilities with which they have been entrusted. In other words, if someone comes to you and needs counsel for a problem, even though you may never have dealt with that problem before, you may suddenly find yourself saying just the right words to help. Or if you are given the opportunity to pray with someone who is sick, even though you've never seen or experienced a miraculous healing, God may heal as you humbly submit to the job at hand. This may only occur once in your lifetime, or it could be experienced on a regular basis. When an individual operates consistently within a particular gift, we might say that he *has* that gift. This is particularly true of apostles, prophets, pastors, evangelists, and teachers, but it could equally apply to all the others who receive gifts.

How do you find your gifts? The best advice I can give you is to quit looking for them! Don't waste a lot of time on introspection and trying to develop a detailed understanding of all the gifts. Instead, ask God to open your eyes to see the needs around you. Trust Him to bring you in contact with the tasks He wants you to

> *Everyone who is willing to work will be given at least one gift.*

do and the people He needs you to help, and then just be willing to follow through. If you don't feel capable, that's fine. Step out on faith. You'll gradually get over the fear of looking foolish. More often than not, you will find that God has used the circumstances of your life to prepare you for the task and that He empowers you with the particular gifts needed at that time.

Sometimes, even after praying about it, you may still not be comfortable taking some action or approaching a specific person. A good solution to this hesitation can be found in the wise old saying, "Give your heart to God, and then follow your heart." In other words, make sure you have no hidden agenda, you're not trying to manipulate a situation, and you're not secretly hoping for others' attention. If you can honestly proceed with a clear conscious, then go ahead. God will honor this type of heart. Even if you were mistaken in the specifics, He will see to it that your actions cause no harm and are used for good.

What about your natural talents and abilities; can they be considered spiritual gifts? Yes. If you make yourself available to be used by God in the service of others, He will guide you in such a way that your natural talents can be used for His glory and His work. Your natural abilities will be magnified and multiplied by the Spirit and will bear spiritual fruit. Somewhere along the way, your talents have become His gifts!

I want to address one final thought on the operation of spiritual gifts. Just as in the church at Corinth, most controversies over the gifts arise from their abuse and misuse. God intends that the gifts be used in the context of a loving, maturing group of believers under good spiritual leadership (Eph. 4:1–6; 1 Pet. 4:7–11; Col. 2:5). In this type of setting, the gifts are used for the good of all, to build up and edify the body of believers. The exuberance of the gifts is balanced by the wisdom of maturity. This analogy is illustrated for us in the Old Testament by the robe of the high priest.

The gifts are used for the good of all, to build up and edify the body of believers.

Bells alternating with pomegranates were sewn around the hem: the bells represent the gifts of the Spirit and the pomegranates represent the fruit of the Spirit. Were the bells placed all together and not tempered by the intervening fruit, they would have produced an awful clanging noise when the priest was executing his duties. With the fruit present, however, the bells made beautiful music. Perhaps this is the picture Paul had in mind when he wrote: "Though I speak with the tongues of men and of angels, but have not love, I have become sounding brass or a clanging cymbal. And though I have the gift of prophecy and understand all mysteries and all knowledge, and though I have all faith, so that I could remove mountains, but have not love, I am nothing. And though I bestow all my goods to feed the poor, and though I give my body to be burned, but have not love, it profits me nothing" (1 Cor. 13:1–3).

Questions for Reflection

1. Why have biblical teachings of the gifts of the Spirit been largely neglected in most mainline churches today?

2. Why is it important that these concepts be taught?

3. Why is it important to allow the free exercise of spiritual gifts?

4. What are the gifts of the Spirit?

5. Who provides these gifts, and how are they to be used?

6. Why do we need "something more" in our personal lives and in our churches?

7. Can the operation of spiritual gifts be practical?

8. Name some scriptural references which address the gifts of the Spirit.

9. Can the gifts of the Spirit be categorized into talents and natural abilities or supernatural manifestations? Why or why not?

10. Why are we more comfortable with some of the gifts than others?

11. Discuss the different gifts and how they are manifested.

12. What is the evidence of the presence of the gifts of the Spirit?

13. What is a common error many fall into regarding the exercise of spiritual gifts in worship services? How can this be avoided?

14. Who can receive these spiritual tools?

15. Who chooses what gifts are given and to whom?

16. Is it okay to ask for a particular gift?

17. How do we find our spiritual gifts?

18. Can your natural talents and abilities be considered spiritual gifts?

19. Can spiritual gifts be misused? How can this be prevented?

✣ Chapter 10 ✣

At Work in the Body

U ntil now, most of this book has focused on the relationship between the Holy Spirit and you as an
individual believer. Now it's time to focus on the
Spirit at work in the body of believers. What is He trying to do
in us, through us, and among us? How is He trying to do it?

Psalm 133 speaks of the beauty of unity among the people
of God:

> Behold, how good and pleasant it is
> For brethren to dwell together in unity!
> It is like the precious oil upon the head,
> Running down on the beard,
> The beard of Aaron,
> Running down on the edge of his garments.
> It is like the dew of Hermon,
> Descending upon the mountains of Zion;
> for there the LORD commanded the blessing—
> Life forevermore.

Moses poured the anointing oil upon Aaron to sanctify
(Lev. 8:12 KJV) or consecrate (Lev. 8:12 NKJV) him for service in
the tabernacle as the high priest. This signified that Aaron was
anointed with the open hand of power, giving him means and
direction for the job, filled with the fullness of that power, and
prepared and purified for God's work.[1]

Oil is used repeatedly throughout the Scriptures to represent the Holy Spirit (James 5:14). Mount Hermon was one of the strongholds of the Anakim (the giants) when Moses and the children of Israel came into the land east of the Jordan River (Josh. 12:4–6). These were of the same race of giants the Israelite spies had seen some forty years previously, the reporting of which caused the older Israelites to doubt and fear, resulting in their failure to march quickly into the land of Canaan as God had prepared (Num. 13:32–14:10).

In Scripture, dew is representative of God's favor and blessing: "The king's . . . favor is like dew on the grass" (Prov. 19:12). Manna in the wilderness came with the dew (Exod. 16:14–15), and "dew of heaven" was a frequently used metaphor in bestowing blessings upon another (Gen. 27:27–29). The mountains of Zion represent Jerusalem and God's dwelling place with man.

What picture is the psalmist trying to paint by comparing unity among the brethren to Aaron's anointing and the dew of Hermon descending upon the mountains of Zion? Our unity in the Holy Spirit is what gives us anointed power and purity, brings victory over our enemies, enables us to possess the land of promise (i.e., the place of rest), and brings God's presence and blessings upon us.

Is it any wonder that Paul admonishes us to endeavor "to keep the unity of the Spirit in the bond of peace" (Eph. 4:1–3)? Unity of the body of believers in the power of the Holy Spirit is not only desirable, it is absolutely essential if we want to have spiritual power, maturity of faith, and victory over Satan.

We come to Christ as individuals, each having to make our own decision to follow Him. But immediately upon our entering His kingdom, we cease to be loners. Our future victories and growth are no longer determined only by our relationship to the Lord, but also and equally by our relationship to our fellow believers. Paul wrote that "God . . . made

us alive *together* with Christ . . . and raised us up *together*,
and made us *sit together* in the heavenly places in Christ Jesus"
(Eph. 2:4–6, emphasis added).

Reading this Scripture one day brought back a memory.
While on a family road trip with our three young sons, my wife
and I soon started hearing a familiar argument from the back
seat of the van. "That's mine, leave it alone!" "You're on my
side, scoot over!" "You're touching me!" "Momma, make him
stop!" "He's breathing my air!"

As usual, we first tried to get them to cooperate with each
other, but the peace would last for only a few miles, then some
variation of the same argument would resume. After awhile I
had reached my limit, and I told the boys, "I don't care who is
doing what to whom! I want you to sit peacefully with each
other. It would be nice if you could get along, and it would
certainly make the trip better for everyone. But if it's the best
you can do, *then just sit there and be quiet!*"

This is essentially the same instruction God gives to us:
". . . walk [*ride*] worthy of the calling with which you were called,
with all lowliness and gentleness, with longsuffering [*patience*],
bearing with one another [*tolerating each other*] in love, endeav-
oring to keep the unity of the Spirit in the bond of peace" (Eph.
4:1–3). Keeping the unity of the Spirit is crucial for a happy ride,
even when it means that we don't get our own way!

Jesus, on the night of His arrest, gave us more insight into
the need for unity among believers. Listen to a portion of His
prayer for us:

> I do not pray for these alone, but also for those who will believe
> in Me through their word; *that they all may be one* as You, Father,
> are in Me, and I in You; *that they also may be one* in Us, that the
> world may believe that You sent Me. And the glory which You
> gave Me I have given them, *that they may be one* just as We are
> one: I in them, and You in Me; *that they may be made perfect in*

> *one*, and that the world may know that You have sent Me, and have loved them as You have loved Me (John 17:20–23, emphasis added).

The greatest witness the church will ever offer the world is through the unity of believers and the way we love and care for each other. The greatest glory we can know this side of heaven is being at one with our brothers and sisters in Christ. It is our love for one another—our being made perfect in oneness, our unity—that presents the clearest picture to those who are lost that God loves them and sent Jesus to die for their sins. Unity is the very essence of the Holy Spirit. He bound the Son on earth to the Father in heaven. He bears witness both on earth and in heaven to the truth of the gospel (1 John 5:7–8). God gives us each other, with a call for unity, as a practical means of maturing in our faith.

The idea of going on to Christian perfection apart from your relationship to other people is foreign to the Scriptures. Jesus speaks of being "perfect" in the context of loving your enemies (Matt. 5:43–48) and giving to the poor (Matt. 18:21), and of course, as noted above, in the context of unity with fellow believers. Jesus was said to have been perfected through the "things which He suffered" (Heb. 5:8–9). He didn't suffer because of Himself; He suffered for us, for our sins. In other words, Jesus was perfected as He obediently poured out Himself for us.

Unity is the very essence of the Holy Spirit.

Paul's clearest teaching about moving toward spiritual perfection is found in the letter to the church at Philippi. While recognizing and confessing that he had not yet attained perfection (Phil. 3:12), he nevertheless understood the means:

Therefore if there is any consolation in Christ, if any comfort of love, if any fellowship of the Spirit, if any affection and mercy, fulfill my joy by being like-minded, having the same love, being of one accord, of one mind. Let nothing be done through selfish ambition or conceit, but in lowliness of mind let each esteem others better than himself. Let each of you look out not only for his own interests, but also for the interests of others. Let this mind be in you which was also in Christ Jesus, who, being in the form of God, did not consider it robbery to be equal with God, but made Himself of no reputation, taking the form of a bondservant, and coming in the likeness of men. And being found in appearance as a man, He humbled Himself and became obedient to the point of death, even the death of the cross (Phil. 2:1–8).

The point is that if you truly desire spiritual growth and perfection, you will seek to serve your fellow man, especially those of the "household of faith" (Gal. 6:10). You will consider others' needs more important than your own. You will be willing to extend any consideration and grace to all. You will be slow to take offense and quick to forgive. There is no way to do this without the body of believers around you. You cannot possibly grow if you become a spiritual hermit with the attitude, *All I need is me, my praise and worship CDs, and the Bible.* It is so tempting to think, *I could be such a strong Christian if I didn't have to put up with all those difficult people in the church!* This is exactly what Satan wants you to believe.

This is precisely why God gives us an objective standard by which we can judge our spiritual growth: "We know that we have passed from death to life, because we love the brethren" (1 John 3:14). This passage doesn't say, ". . . because we love the brethren who are easy to get along with and don't rub us the wrong way!" Let me reiterate: We need each other!

It's as if we're all thrown into a big rock tumbler together. God uses your rough edges to knock off my rough edges. If we persevere and grow, if we yield ourselves to the supremacy of Christ, if we give up our right to be right, if we put Christ in control, if we don't "bail out" of the tumbler because it hurts a little to stay in there, we will eventually all be poured out smoothed, polished, and perfected. If nobody ever offends you, how are you going to learn forgiveness? If nobody ever corrects you, how far will you stray? If you're never tested, how will your faith grow? If you never see yourself in somebody else's mirror, how can you spot the imperfections?

> *It is so tempting to think,* I could be such a strong Christian if I didn't have to put up with all those difficult people in the church!

This may sound a little tough, but the promise is sure. If you give up your stuff and I give up my stuff and we seek God together, we will be rewarded with "joy inexpressible and full of glory, receiving the end of your faith—the salvation [*full restoration*] of your souls" (1 Pet. 1:8–9). We'll never have everything figured out just exactly right. Even if we did, we wouldn't always do it right anyway. Our knowledge of Scripture and doctrine will never be perfect. Our efforts in ministry and the use of spiritual gifts will fall short. But the one overriding promise of Scripture is ". . . love will cover a multitude of sins" (1 Pet. 4:8).

It is no wonder that Satan works so hard at causing disunity in the church. Disunity is the antithesis of the Holy Spirit. Since unity is our greatest witness and our greatest protection, if Satan can entice us to quarrel and bicker, the resultant disunity quenches the Spirit, nullifies our witness, and opens a crack in our protection. This is why Paul told the Corinthian church, "Now whom you forgive anything, I also forgive. For if indeed I have forgiven anything, I have forgiven that one for your sakes in the presence of Christ, lest Satan should take advantage of us; for we are not ignorant of his devices" (2 Cor. 2:10–11).

Paul reminds us that unity and harmony are essential if we are truly glorifying God: "And do not grieve the Holy Spirit of God, by whom you were sealed for the day of redemption. Let all bitterness, wrath, anger, clamor, and evil speaking be put away from you, with all malice. And be kind to one another, tenderhearted, forgiving one another, even as God in Christ forgave you" (Eph. 4:30–32).

Questions for Reflection

1. Why did Moses anoint Aaron with oil and what did this signify?

2. What (or who) does anointing oil represent?

3. What picture is painted by comparing unity among the brethren to Aaron's anointing and the dew of Hermon descending upon the mountains of Zion?

4. Why is this unity among the brethren vitally important?

5. What instruction does God give us in Ephesians 4:1–3?

6. What is the greatest witness the church can offer the world?

7. Why is unity such a powerful witness?

8. Whom does the Holy Spirit bind together?

9. According to Hebrews 5:6–9, how was Jesus perfected?

10. How can we press on toward perfection (spiritual growth) in a similar manner?

11. How do we know that we have passed from death into life?

12. What promises are given in 1 Peter 1:8–9 and 1 Peter 4:8 and what must we do to secure them?

Chapter 11

The Simplicity of the Gospel

T he gospel of Jesus Christ is not complicated. The infinite God, in His wisdom, has taken the most complicated of matters and simplified it to an extent that any thinking human being can comprehend and appropriate. Paul, knowing the human tendency to be drawn to mystery and hidden knowledge, was concerned that we might easily be enticed away from this simplicity (2 Cor. 11:3). Lest I be guilty of making things too complicated in this book, I want to provide a very succinct summation of the major themes:

- **Who is the Holy Spirit?**
  He is the Spirit of the risen Christ who lives in us and works through and among us who have accepted Jesus as Lord and Savior. He is the manifestation of God who works intimately with all of creation.

- **What does it mean to be born of the Spirit?**
  It simply means that which was dead in you (your spirit) because of sin has been made alive by the One who has the power to give you Life. His name is Jesus the Christ, the Son of the Living God. Your sins are forgiven, and your separation from God has ended.

- **What does it mean to be baptized with the Spirit?**
  Baptism means to be "immersed into" or "completely covered." Baptism in the Holy Spirit is not about your having all of the Spirit, but about submitting all of yourself to Him.

- **What does it mean to walk in the Spirit?**
  Walking in the Spirit means to be led by the Spirit every day in all matters, both large and small. At each and every moment, we will either be motivated by the old nature or the new. If we say "no" to our selfish tendencies and "yes" to God, the Spirit immediately provides us the strength to live out the choices of our will. He will never make the choices for us, and we can never live as we ought without His strength.

- **What are the gifts of the Holy Spirit?**
  The gifts of the Spirit are tools given by God to the church, distributed to and operating through individual members of the body, to do the work that God wants and needs done. They are essential if we really want to be the body of Christ on Earth.

- **Why is unity in the church so essential?**
  Unity is the essence of the Holy Spirit. Unity is our greatest witness to the world and our best protection against the schemes of Satan. The unity the Spirit brings is not one based on compromise, but one based on Scripture and truth and worked out through each member in dying to self.

I hope my sharing on the Holy Spirit has been enlightening. I pray that a layman's perspective, while not theologically challenging, may nevertheless be clear and meaningful. Living life in the Holy Spirit is about having the wisdom to make the right choices and the strength to follow them. It's about everyday living. It's about finding the power for living victoriously, not letting life's adversities get you down. It's about knowing and experiencing the love and power of God each day. I wouldn't want anybody to think that I have all this figured out completely or that I can apply it flawlessly; I certainly don't and continue to have my own struggles and growing pains. But I do know in whom I believe and am determined to press on!

The psalmist declares: "Oh, taste and see that the Lord is good. Blessed is the man who trusts in Him" (Ps. 34:8). Are you willing to trust Him? You must know that whatever He has prepared for you is for your good. He loves you enough that He died for you; He died so you could spend eternity with Him. The moment you accept Jesus as Savior, you enter eternal life. His Holy Spirit seals you and becomes your own little

> *Living life in the Holy Spirit is about having the wisdom to make the right choices and the strength to follow them.*

bit of heaven to take with you. Let Jesus fill you with His Spirit and begin the most exciting journey you could ever hope to imagine! God bless!

Questions for Reflection

1. Who is the Holy Spirit?

2. What does it mean to be born of the Spirit?

3. What does it mean to be baptized with the Spirit?

4. What does it mean to walk in the Spirit?

5. What are the gifts of the Spirit?

6. Why is unity in the church so essential?

Epilogue by Jackie Ragland
"Lord, I Believe . . ."

My husband Don has asked me to conclude this study by giving my personal testimony of the work of the Holy Spirit in my life and in our marriage. I'll begin by referencing one of my favorite passages of Scripture: the story of the man whose son was demon-possessed. He came to our Lord and His disciples in the fervent hope of finding help and health for his loved one. After the disciples failed to rid the boy of this demon, the father approached Jesus asking Him to have compassion on his son. "Jesus said to him, 'If you can believe, all things are possible to him who believes.' Immediately the father of the child cried out and said with tears, 'Lord, I believe; help my unbelief!'" (Mark 9:24). This has been my cry for many years during times of trouble.

As alluded to earlier, the first years of our marriage were, like so many, troublesome. To the outside world, ours was a picture-perfect marriage. However, Don had immersed himself in the business of veterinary medicine, and I was surrounded by the grayness of depression. We had somehow grown apart and were so buried in our daily routines that without knowing how or why, we had become strangers.

Both of us had prayed from our early teenage years that the Lord would bring into our lives His choice for a mate. We knew early in our relationship (although we were very young) that He had done just that. We knew that this had been His will for our lives, yet something just wasn't right. Once again, I found myself crying out to our Lord, "Lord, I believe; help my unbelief!" His answer, given in His perfect timing, was far greater than I expected.

Slowly He began to work on both of us, softening Don's heart and drawing Don closer to Him, while bringing peace to my heart and determination to stay put, despite difficult circumstances. Don began to study the Word closely on a daily basis, often staying up until two or three o'clock in the morning. We were approached about attending a weekend program called the Walk to Emmaus. The Lord used this program in a mighty way to change many problems in our lives, drawing us closer to Him and, therefore, closer to each other. It was during this program that we both came to be filled (or baptized) with the Holy Spirit, although at the time we had no idea what had happened or even what to call this strange phenomenon. All we knew was that we were suddenly no longer the same people we had been a few weeks before!

The Lord blessed us with an instantaneous healing.

Before long, others began to notice a difference as well. Don's teaching in Sunday school class, while very good beforehand, became obviously anointed, touching and changing the lives of those in attendance. In fact, before long we were known as a very nice young couple who were just a bit too "radical" in our beliefs. Our picture-perfect marriage on the outside was likewise totally healed on the inside. Our faith became "Rock"-solid (Jesus being the Rock, the Cornerstone), and we began to see tremendous growth in our understanding of both the Scriptures we read and the people around us. This wisdom and understanding enabled us to minister to the many hurting people whom the Lord would bring into our lives.

Not long afterward, we discovered that our second child was on the way. However, during the ninth week of my pregnancy, I developed a problem called placenta previa, a condition which causes loss of blood due to pressure on the cervix—and often causes miscarriage. I was instructed not to worry, but to be sure to get to the hospital should the bleeding increase greatly—much easier said than done!

At the nineteenth week of pregnancy, I was feeling quite anemic and physically drained. My doctor had given me one more week and then was going to prescribe total bed rest for the remainder of my pregnancy—not an easy task when there is a three-year-old at home.

I asked some close friends (who were then, and continue to be, Spirit-filled) to pray for me, and the Lord blessed us with an instantaneous healing. In that moment, I felt the pressure leave. My child gave a tremendous kick (the first of many)—and the bleeding stopped from that point on.

During the seventh month of this same pregnancy, the Lord again graced me with another physical healing, this time of my left hip, which frequently popped out of place due to a half-inch difference in the length of my legs. Both of these incidences were difficult for my scientifically trained husband to reconcile—or to deny! These are but two of many instances of healing we have witnessed and/or experienced throughout the years.

We have also been blessed in many other ways. There have been times while in ministry when one or both of us have been given words of wisdom, words of knowledge, or prophetic words. We have been honored to minister to those who are oppressed, either spiritually or emotionally. People have literally shown up at our doorstep with no idea of why they were there or what was wrong; they just knew that they were hurting and in need of prayer. We have been witnesses to deliverances, engaged in spiritual warfare, and continued in other aspects of ministry and spiritual growth.

Our church family has also been greatly blessed as we have together come to see the need for similar spiritual growth within our corporate church body. Where there once was strife and pettiness, there is now a striving for unity and peace. Where there once was a sense of isolation among our members, there is now a sense of family. Where there once was a sense of apathy toward spiritual growth, there is now hunger. Like all churches, ours is a collection of flawed human beings. We make our share of mistakes, but we have come to recognize the absolute necessity for being both filled with and led by the Holy Spirit in order to worship Him in spirit and in truth—which is to have life! We are not perfect, but we are going on toward perfection in accordance with His Word.

As you have read and studied this little book, you may have discovered a yearning for something more within your life. Please understand that we believe God does not expect us to be perfect, but rather urges us to grow and move on toward perfection. We cannot do this in our own strength, but we *can* choose to lay down our lives on a daily basis and give Him permission to bring about these changes in us.

Should you find yourself with this longing, first rejoice and give Him thanks, for this is evidence of His great love for you and the reality of your life in Him. Ask Him for guidance as you grow and study His Word, your most reliable authority on any subject. Pray for Him to bring into your life people who can help you in this endeavor. Seek out His body of believers as you seek to grow (remember, none of us are Lone Rangers). Ask Him to give you spiritual eyes in order to see where He is at work around you, and then join Him in that work. Make prayer an unceasing habit. Ask Him to bring into your life someone to whom He would have you minister and the wisdom and ability to minister to them, having faith that He will answer your prayer in wondrous ways. Be sure *always* to give Him the praise and the glory in all that you do and in all He is doing in and through you.

My prayer for you is that this study will demystify some of the many misconceptions surrounding the person and work of the Holy Spirit, that it will encourage you to reach beyond your present understanding (your comfort zone), and that you, too, will be blessed beyond measure as you walk closer to Him! Our Lord is both merciful and mighty. He is also a gentleman, and will not lead you into anything that will bring you harm.

> *We have come to recognize the absolute necessity for being both filled with and led by the Holy Spirit in order to worship Him in spirit and in truth— which is to have life!*

✠

"Oh taste and see that the LORD is good!" (Ps. 34:8). The work He does in our lives is only limited by how much and what *we* believe *He* can do. Therein lies the cry, "Lord, I believe; help my unbelief!"

⋈ *Notes* ⋈

Chapter 3
1. Halford E. Luccock, Paul Hutchinson, and Robert W. Goodloe, *The Story of Methodism* (Nashville, Tenn.: Abingdon Press, 1926), 189.

Chapter 4
1. Gordon S. Jackson, *Quotes for the Journey, Wisdom for the Way* (Colorado Springs, Colo.: NavPress, 2000), 70.
2. James Strong, LL.D., S.T.D., *Strong's Exhaustive Concordance of the Bible* (Nashville, Tenn.: Thomas Nelson, Inc., 1995), Greek no. 907, 16.

Chapter 5
1. Watchman Nee, *The Spiritual Man*, vol. 1 (New York, N.Y.: Christian Fellowship Publishers, Inc., 1968), 84.
2. Ibid., 89.

Chapter 6
1. J. I. Packer, *Knowing God* (Downers Grove, Ill.: InterVarsity Press, 1973), 206.
2. Fuchsia Pickett, SheKinah Ministries, Blountville, Tenn., cassette tape, unnamed and undated.
3. Why the age thirty? Under Judaic law, future priests would begin their formal training at the age of twenty, but did not begin service until the age of thirty. Jesus was being obedient to the law and custom (see Numbers 4).

Chapter 7
1. Robertson McQuilken, *Life in the Spirit* (Nashville, Tenn.: Broadman and Holman, 2000), 154.
2. Ibid., 155.
3. The term "supernatural" is used here to simply mean something above and beyond the natural abilities of man.

Chapter 8
1. Andrew Murray, *Abide in Christ* (New Kensington, Pa.: Whitaker House, 1979), 20–21.

Chapter 10
1. James Strong, L.L.D., S.T.D., *Strong's Exhaustive Concordance of the Bible* (Nashville, Tenn.: Thomas Nelson, Inc., 1995), Hebrew no. 3027, 4390, 6942.

❧ *Bibliography* ❧

Jackson, Gordon S. *Quotes for the Journey, Wisdom for the Way.* Colorado Springs, Colo.: NavPress, 2000.

Luccock, Halford E., Paul Hutchinson, and Robert W. Goodloe. *The Story of Methodism.* Nashville, Tenn.: Abingdon Press, 1926.

McQuilken, Robertson. *Life in the Spirit.* Nashville, Tenn.: Broadman and Holman, 2000.

Murray, Andrew. *Abide in Christ.* New Kensington, Pa.: Whitaker House, 1979.

Nee, Watchman. *The Spiritual Man.* New York, N.Y.: Christian Fellowship Publishers, Inc., 1968.

Packer, J. I. *Knowing God.* Downers Grove, Ill.: InterVarsity Press, 1973.

Pickett, Fuchsia, SheKinah Ministries, Blountville, Tenn.

Strong, James. *Strong's Exhaustive Concordance of the Bible.* Nashville, Tenn.: Thomas Nelson, Inc., 1995.

✣ *About the Authors* ✣

D on and Jackie Ragland share a passion for seeing the Holy Spirit at work in His people. They have dedicated their adult lives to knowing Him and being led by Him. It is their hope that their experiences with God will encourage others to come to know the power, love, and fire of the person of the Holy Spirit at work in their lives.

Donald Ragland, D.V.M., is a full-time veterinarian in general practice in Livingston, Tennessee. He completed his undergraduate work at Tennessee Technological University before earning a doctor of veterinary medicine degree from the University of Tennessee College of Veterinary Medicine.

Jackie Ragland works as a payroll administrator and licensed practical nurse. A native of Salt Lake City, Utah, she attended Tennessee Technological University and earned her practical nursing certification from Tennessee Technology Center at Livingston.

The Raglands have been married since 1976 and reside in Cookeville, Tennessee. They have three children, Eric, Paul, and Jared, married to Niquie.